TIME FOR COLLEGE

also by Al Siebert:

Student Success: How to Succeed in College and Still Have Time for Your Friends (co-author: Timothy L. Walter)
The Adult Student's Guide to Success in College, (co-author: Timothy L. Walter)
Involvement in Psychology Today
Learning Psychology, (co-author: Timothy L. Walter)

also by Bernadine Gilpin:

Career Cycles 1: Job Loss/Change
Career Cycles 2: Right Job For You
Career Cycles 3: Get Job Information
Career Cycles 4: Résumés, Application
Career Cycles 5: Interviews

TIME
FOR
COLLEGE

When you work, have a family,
and want more from life

AL SIEBERT & BERNADINE GILPIN

Contributing editors:

Samuel Kimball, University of North Florida
Regina Myers, Northeast Missouri State University
Timothy Walter, University of Michigan

Foreword and comments by Mary Karr

Illustrations by Teresa Rosen

Practical Psychology Press
Portland, Oregon

Practical Psychology Press
P.O.Box 535
Portland, Oregon 97207

Library of Congress Catalog Card Number: 88-63617

ISBN 0-944227-01-5

Book design by Susan Applegate of Publishers Bookworks, Inc.

To all our students
who had the courage and commitment
to pursue their dreams.

FOREWORD

I did it! I graduated from college with honors and I've now completed a graduate degree. ME! With a husband, four children, three dogs, a cat, and a 44-mile commute each day.

Do you feel nervous? Wonder if you will be able to study and pass tests? Concerned about the effect that your going to college will have on your family? Worried that your car may break down one morning? Feel like you won't fit in? If so, then you know how all the rest of us felt when we first started!

Time For College will give you the kind of practical information that usually comes only through experience. It will help you develop effective study habits and good test-taking skills. It will give you lots of information about how to get through the institutional maze, information that helps you avoid the costly time and money mistakes that can frustrate anyone. It will be invaluable for you.

Mostly, I would say that if you believe in yourself, and take things one day at a time, you can get the education you've dreamed about. You have faced up to tough challenges before. You can survive late nights studying, taking tests, and writing papers. With good effort your chances are very good that you can succeed in college. If I did it, I believe you can too!

Mary Karr

CONTENTS

Chapter 1

Going to College: Dreams for a Better Future

Have you thought about all of the benefits you will gain by going to college after years away from school?

Do you know that at many colleges the average age is about 30 and that over half of the students work while going to school?

Do you know that there are no age restrictions on financial aid? That you can get financial aid even as a part-time student?

Do you know about all the services, help, and support available to you at colleges and universities?

Your Gateway to the Future

If you dream of a better future for yourself, going to college is one of the best ways to get there. Starting college can be like stepping through a gateway into a new world and a better life.

Going to college is not without its problems, however....

Some Normal Fears and Concerns

Do you feel fearful about going to college? Concerned that your brain is rusty and that you won't be able to keep up with younger students? Are you afraid that you can't afford college and yet don't see how you could work and go to college and raise your family? Feel guilty about depriving your family while you do something that feels selfish?

Welcome to the club! *You are normal.* Most older college students felt the same fears and concerns when they started. Yet they are succeeding in college and having the time of their lives!

How *Time For College* Will Help You

Every chapter in the book contains valuable information about how to succeed in college when you have been away from school for awhile, may have a family, and probably have to work.

The first chapters cover how to get started. **Chapter 2** shows how to *confront and eliminate many fears and concerns* reported by older than average students.

Chapter 3 explains *how to make enrollment easy.* Most students need some form of financial assistance, so this chapter includes information on *how to obtain finance your education.*

Part of being successful in new situations is to locate the resources available to you. **Chapter 4** provides information about how to locate the *many sources of help available* at your college.

Most college students aged 25 or older have families. In **Chapter 5** you will find many practical ways to gain *cooperation, support, and encouragement from your family.*

Chapter 6 shows *how to combine working with taking college courses.* Most students work. You may be amazed at how many employers offer special work schedules and reimbursement for courses completed. This chapter also has suggestions on what to do if you need a "bread and butter" job.

The middle chapters are devoted to passing your courses with high grades. **Chapter 7** clarifies *differences between successful and unsuccessful students.*

All of your responsibilities require *effective time management.* **Chapter 8** shows you how to make good use of the limited time that you have available.

Chapter 9 provides practical information about how to study using *the best, most widely used, effective study method.* Here you will learn how to reach a study goal, stop studying, and reward yourself. Self-motivated people have to learn how to be self-stoppers!

Nervous about taking tests? **Chapter 10** shows you *how to prepare for tests* so that you feel confident, less nervous, and score higher than you suspected you could.

Term papers are always a challenge. In **Chapter 11** you will find an excellent way to *write papers that get high grades.*

The last chapters provide information and guidelines about how to cope with challenges of college and life in general. **Chapter 12** prepares you for some predictable conflicts that arise between students and instructors. In this chapter and in **Chapter 13** you will find guidelines on *how to resolve the conflicts* and how to *influence your instructors.*

Going to college has its stresses and strains. **Chapter 14** contains a simple but effective way to *minimize stresses* and increase your revitalizing experiences.

In many ways life itself is the real school. **Chapter 15** is based on research into the personalities of people who are best at surviving life's adversities. The way to *develop a survivor personality* is with self-managed learning in the school of life.

At the end of each chapter you will find an **Action Review**. It is a checklist for reviewing how well you are putting into action what the chapter covered.

Many students come to college searching for new or better careers. Other students already know what they want and are in a career development program. We decided to place *career infor-*

mation in **Appendix A**. If you are searching for a career, Appendix A will be helpful.

Bernadine started college after raising a family. Al was raised by a working mother who went to school to learn a new career. If you'd like to read about our experiences read **Appendix B**, The Authors Talk.

Dreams and Clocks

In this first chapter we would like to introduce you to a little character that Bernadine named "OTA." OTA was created for us by Terry Rosen. The initials stand for "older than average," a designation given by many colleges to students such as yourself who did not go directly from high school to college.

We wanted to use an animated clock in the book because when your dream for a better future includes taking college courses you need clocks. Clocks and dreams do not generally go well together but in college you get up, eat, leave for school, arrive for class, study, and return home by the clock.

If you have children, work, and other important responsibilities you live by the clock from morning until night. Clocks help you reach your dream of a college education and a better life. We hope that OTA makes your journey more interesting.

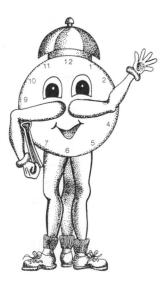

Consider Forming a College Success Group

Many older students feel isolated and friendless at first. As a new college student you have a permission to approach other students. We want to encourage you to find two or three other students to join with you in creating a college success support group.

You will find guidelines for getting started at the end of this chapter. Exchange telephone numbers. Plan to meet frequently during the first few weeks of school, then perhaps less often after you settle in. Every chapter ends with suggested topics or issues to discuss in your college success group.

You are Special as a Student

Have you noticed that when you tell people about going to college to pursue a new career, they treat you differently? Mary Karr, who wrote the Foreword for us, started college shortly after her youngest daughter entered high school. Mary recalls this immediate change in how people treated her:

> Before I started college, when my husband and I went to a party or social gathering , people would ask what I did. When I told them I was a housewife raising four children they'd say, "Oh," and start talking to someone else. On a scale from 1 to 100, I felt like I rated about a 3, just above politician and used car salesman. After I enrolled, when people found out I was a college student, they'd say, "Oh!" Their eyes lighted up, and I got treated like I had something important to say. My rating soared to the high nineties. The difference was fantastic!

The World Wants You to Succeed

Going to college is an exciting challenge. It will take hard work and some sacrifices but the benefits are worth the effort. The main point to understand is that you are not alone. There are many people and many resources available to you. The world wants you to succeed in your effort to better yourself and better your life!

Success Group Activity: Getting A Group Started

Here are some guidelines for starting a College Success Group:

- Get together with a few other beginning students. Urge one or two new students that seem "lost" to come along.
- Plan on being together for an hour or longer.
- Meet in a place where you can sit comfortably and talk easily with each other. The cafeteria, for example, is a place where, as students, you can sit and talk for hours.
- Inroduce yourselves. Keep repeating and checking that you have each other's names right as you talk and listen.
- Take turns talking about your feeling, impressions, and experiences starting college.
- Do not let one person dominate the sharing of feelings and experiences. Take turns.
- Find out why you each decided to go to college. Ask about difficulties that have to be handled.
- Talk about your dreams and plans for the future. What do you each hope to be doing three or four years from now?
- Ask about the courses you've signed up for. Find out what programs you have selected or are considering.
- Make certain that each person feels heard. Make sure that by the time you finish each of you has the feeling "A few of my classmates know about me and understand what I am feeling and experiencing."
- Exchange telephone numbers.
- Agree on when you will meet again. During the first weeks it will be useful to meet frequently. Then shift to less frequent meetings as you settle in.
- Congratulate and hug each other for having the courage to take this very important step in life.

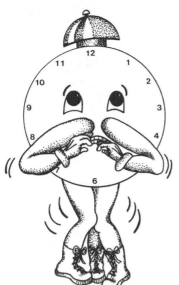

Chapter 2

Fears and Concerns: How to Confront and Overcome Them

Has it occurred to you that some of your fears about going to college may not be realistic?

Do you know that instructors like older students in their classes and that older students get better grades?

Do you know that financial aid is available to older and part-time students?

Do you know that colleges, universities, and company training programs are eager for participants and go out of their way to help students succeed?

The Greatest Fear...

Have you overcome fears in the past by facing up to them? By looking closely at fears and seeking information about what was worrying you, you have probably found out how unrealistic many of them really were. The same principle applies here.

In this book we will show you how thousands of people just like you have overcome their fears and succeeded in college. We will show you how to develop the skills you need to build your confidence. We will show you how to locate and use resources that you never knew existed.

If you have not studied or taken tests for a long time, have to work, and perhaps also raise a family, you may doubt your ability to succeed in college. You needn't be anxious about combining your present lifestyle with that of a successful student. You can improve your learning skills and still handle other daily responsibilities. But first, let's take some time to deal with some fears expressed by older students.

Common Fears and Concerns of OTA Students

Take a look at the following list of fears and concerns. If you have felt or thought any of them, you are typical of most returning students. As you read the list, ask yourself, "Does this fear or concern make me worry about not succeeding in school?" and "Am I being realistic?"

I haven't studied in years. I'm out of practice. My brain feels rusty.
> Reality: There is no evidence that older students can't learn and remember as well as younger students. This book will show you how to take notes, remember information from lectures and texts, and pass tests as well as any younger student.

I'm not sure I can read, write, or do math well enough to take college courses.
> Reality: The college is happy to give you a free assessment of your skill levels to advise you what courses are best suited for you. If you need brush-up courses they are available.

Young students seem so smart. I feel dumb around them. They learn fast and understand quickly.

Reality: Young students are also nervous about being successful in college classes. Young students often view older students as wiser, as tough competition.

I won't be able to compete. Only a few smart students receive high grades.

Reality: Instructors seldom grade in a way that causes students to fail. Most instructors want all their students to succeed in their courses. When you show your instructors that you have learned the subject, you are likely to receive a good grade.

They won't let me enroll because I don't have a high-school diploma.

Reality: They will let you enroll and you don't need a diploma to take courses at most community colleges. You can take tests called *equivalency tests* to earn a certificate, which is the same as a high-school diploma. If you want to learn, many schools won't even ask if you have a diploma.

When my daughter applied to different colleges, they all asked for her SAT or ACT scores. There's no way I could do well enough on the college entrance exams to qualify.

Reality: The Scholastic Aptitude Test (SAT) and American College Test (ACT) are given to high-school seniors to see how they compare with each other in basic scholastic skills. Older-than-average students do not have to submit these tests scores. The academic assessment offered free by colleges takes the place of these nationally conducted tests.

I won't fit in. I will be an outsider in a world much different from my own.

Reality: You have as much right to be in school as anyone else. In fact, your tax dollars may have helped build the place. The students, faculty, and administrative members of any college will be far more friendly and helpful than you ever imagined. Many younger students enjoy having older friends from whom they can learn and exchange views and experiences.

Instructors won't like having older students in their classes.

Reality: You are close in age to many instructors and have a lot in common with them. Most instructors enjoy and welcome older students. These instructors welcome the life experience many older students offer to a class. They find that communication is easier with you. Many instructors will tell you that they would rather teach older students than those just out of high school. Returning students often are more motivated to learn and pay closer attention to the instructor than do younger students. Studies show that older students tend to get better grades than younger students.

I was so nervous the first day of classes that I arrived at school 45 minutes ahead of the 9:00 class time. It was OK though, because I needed the time to keep running into the rest room—bladders seem so insistent sometimes. As I walked into the room for my first class I realized that my legs were shaking so hard I could barely walk. Fortunately, the front seat nearest the door was available so I quickly sat down. I tried to remain calm, but I knew I was trembling—my hands just wouldn't stop. After a *very* long time, the teacher came in and was ready to start the class. The first thing I noticed was how young she was and I thought to myself that school was going to be harder than I had imagined because how could this very young woman (she looked like a student herself) ever understand someone my age. Then I noticed that her legs were shaking! *She was nervous! Wonderful!* My day changed and was grand from then on. Oh yes,— I also found out that she was a graduate teaching assistant and that she was very sympathetic to all students. —MK

I was always nervous taking tests. I'll be too upset to do well.

This book is designed to show you how to prepare for and take tests without getting overly anxious. Most college counseling or study skill centers provide help for students who need to learn techniques of test taking. Ask around. Expert help is available.

I can't afford college.

Reality: Most students qualify for some sort of financial aid. This may be in the form of scholarships, loans, grants, or employer reimbursements. And did you know that programs now exist where you can earn college credit for working? We will go into this in more detail in Chapter 3. College administrators and counselors are well aware of the financial dilemmas facing returning students and will assist you in obtaining aid.[1]

I'm retired, I'd like to attend a few classes but I can't afford to pay tuition.

Reality: Many state-supported schools allow senior citizens to attend classes at little or no charge, if space is available. If you are over 65, you can get a college degree at very low cost.

I have young children to raise, and can't afford the cost of child care. Most courses are taught during the day. How can I attend class while I have children to care for?

Reality: Colleges are accommodating the needs of returning students. Many campuses offer low-cost child-care services for students. Colleges are doing everything possible to assist people who work and/or who have children. Most colleges offer classes at night and on weekends. Courses can be taken at home during the day by watching broadcasts on public television. Some courses are available on video tapes at a learning center where you go through the material at your own speed, at a time that is convenient to you. Correspondence or home study courses could also be an option.

It will take me years to earn a degree, since I cannot attend full time. How can I possibly take that long to finish a degree program?

Reality: A long journey starts with the first step. Once you become adjusted to being a student and gain more confidence, you will probably be able to take more courses each term. Some colleges let you "challenge" basic courses. If you pass the proficiency test, you get credit for the course without having to take it. In some cases, your life experiences and skills can be counted as credit toward your degree. Or, you might consider a shorter program. Many colleges offer two-year programs for people training to become nurses or dietitians, for example. Regardless of the program you take, most students report their college careers go much faster than they had ever thought possible.

My family will suffer. I will have to spend so much time with schoolwork that my family will feel rejected. What if my partner and/or friends feel threatened by my attempt to improve myself?

Reality: Your family and friends are quite capable of supporting you in your new role as a student. It's up to you to explain to your family why you need to return to school. Show your family how your success will benefit all of you. Give your family a chance and they will probably support you. Chapter 5 has a number of practical suggestions.

My past history in school is not good. I'm afraid they won't let me in.

Reality: Most community colleges and career training schools have an open door policy. They care only about what you can do now. You may be happy to know that after accumulating 30 or more hours credit at a community college, most four-year colleges and universities will let you transfer in.

I have a heavy load at work and it's not getting any lighter. I'd never have time to take courses. I would have too many pressures.

Reality: Saying that you'd never have time is realistic only if you're unwilling to give up an evening a week to take a course. Employers are often willing to adjust workloads for employees in college, see Chapter 6. The time management tips in Chapter 8 will help. For guidelines on dealing with stress and pressure, read Chapter 14. The solution is to decide what you want in life and go for it.

If I become a student, I'll never have time for my family, friends, or outside interests. I can't take courses, study, and still have time for anything else.

Reality: Millions of people have gone to college while working, raising children, and maintaining active personal lives.

You are no different. If you follow the guidelines for succeeding in school, you'll do just fine and still have time for non-student life.

Where There's a Will...

As you can see, many of your worries about being a college student are unrealistic. As you have probably found from past experience, fears usually disappear when you confront them.

Here are the steps to follow:

1. Clarify the worry. Be very specific about exactly what it is. Write it down or try to explain it to someone who is a good listener.
2. Ask yourself, "Is my worry based on hearsay, rumors, or opinions, or is it a result of known facts?"
3. To deal with potential problems and difficulties that might occur, (a) ask people who have been through it about their experiences, and (b) get first-hand experience to find out if your fears are real.
4. With real problems, seek the advice of experts and develop a realistic plan of action for improving or solving the problem. Don't be afraid to ask questions.

Colleges, Universities, and Company Training Programs Want You

In the last few years a change has taken place in higher education. Colleges and company training programs are doing many things to attract and keep older students.

Colleges arrange financial aid, employment, transportation (car pools and buses), housing, child care, personal counseling, medical coverage, and classes on how to study efficiently and pass courses. They provide counselors and advisors, recreational activities, and much more. They want to attract and retain students. Likewise, companies will often pay trainees to go through a training program, provide fringe benefits, and guarantee jobs to graduates.

Now is the best time in history to obtain a college education. Colleges, universities, and various organizations have excellent training facilities, expensive training equipment, and high calibre teachers waiting for students who want an education and advanced skills.

Action Review

Using the following numbers, indicate how strong or weak your fear is about the following.

Strong—5 Moderately strong—4 Medium—3 Mild—2 Weak—1

1. __ I can't compete with younger students.
2. __ I won't be able to learn, my brain is rusty.
3. __ I can't do well in math.
4. __ I won't be able to study well.
5. __ Instructors dislike older students.
6. __ I won't fit in.
7. __ I won't have time for my family or other interests.
8. __ I don't have a high school diploma.
9. __ I can't afford college.
10. __ I can't work and study and raise a family.
11. __ Going part time will take me too long.
12. __ My family will suffer.

Success Group Activity

Talk with each other about your fears and concerns. Then discuss how you can overcome or eliminate the fears and barriers. Keep in mind, too, that some problems can't be eliminated but it helps to talk about them with people who understand.

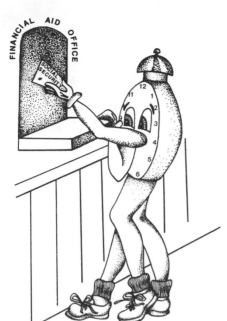

Chapter 3

Enrolling and Financing Made Easier

Do you know how to enroll in college? What information to take with you?

Do you understand the difference between credit and noncredit courses?

Have you heard that you can turn some of your life experiences into college credit?

Do you know where to inquire about financial aid?

Do you know that you can probably get financial aid if you need it?

Getting Enrolled

Enrolling at a two-year community college or technical college is different than enrolling at a four-year college or university.

At a four-year college or university, you must apply for admission and meet certain admission requirements before they will let you enroll.

Most community and technical colleges have an open door policy. You do not have to meet admissions requirements. No matter what your background they will have some classes for you. It is possible to just show up, select the courses you want to take, fill out the registration forms, and pay tuition fees.

If you want to enroll in a specific vocational, technical, or degree program, however, we recommend that you speak to an advisor. It may be necessary to go through an assessment of your reading, writing, and math skills. If you need basic skill classes, the advisors and career counselors will help you arrange to take them, usually at no cost.

Community college and technical college classes can lead to a two-year associate degree but the courses you take may or may not transfer to a university for a four-year degree. If you don't know what you want, check with the counseling or advising office. It's a free service and they'll help you.

Credit, Noncredit, and Transfer Courses

The first thing to do is obtain a copy of the college catalog. Take your time looking through it. Learn how to tell the difference between a credit course, a non-credit course, and a transfer course. A *non-credit* course is not counted toward a four-year college degree. A *credit* course leads to a degree or certificate. You cannot earn a college degree by taking non-credit courses. A *transfer* course is a credit course that will be accepted by most four-year colleges if you want to transfer.

You'll need to know what's ahead of you and what courses you will have to take. Your catalog describes all the courses available and tells you which ones you will be required to take if you want a degree or certificate. Read the fine print carefully.

☆ NOTE: *The school catalog is a kind of contract.* The school agrees to award you a degree if you do all the required work. Keep a copy for future reference.

If a course sounds interesting but is within a program for people majoring in that area, you might have to take a prerequisite course before taking the one you wish. A *prerequisite* course is one that students must take and complete before they can get into a more advanced course. Some courses are so popular there are many classes during the day with many instructors. If you have a choice, find out which instructors students recommend and why they recommend them. Keep in mind that an easy course may not be the best for you.

Program Choices

You will need to decide how many courses and how many credit hours you want to try. A full-time student usually takes four or five courses totalling from 12 to 17 credit hours. The college will have a policy limiting the number of hours a student can take.

If you take two or three courses you will be a half-time student, depending on the total of the credit hour.

To help clarify the program choices facing you, here is a short summary of the vocational and academic programs available at most community colleges:

Associate Degrees — Require about two years taking a full load.
  • General Studies—a combination of vocational courses, transfer courses, and basic skill building courses.
  • Vocational—examples: nursing, diesel mechanics, dental assistant, computer science, television.
  • Arts/Humanities—courses in writing, journalism, music, speech communications, theater arts (courses that transfer into four year degree programs at degree granting colleges or universities).
  • Science—examples: biology, botany, chemistry, geology, math, computer science (transfer courses).
  • Social Science—examples: psychology, sociology, political

science, history, geography, economics, women's studies (humanities and arts transfer courses.)

Transfer courses taken at a community college or enrollment at a four year college can lead to the following academic degress:

Bachelor of Arts (B.A.) —Earned in a four year program emphasizing humanities and arts courses plus a foreign language at an accredited college or university.

Bachelor of Science (B.S.) —Earned in a four year program emphsizing science courses plus advance level mathematics at an accredited college or university.

Master of Arts (M.A.) or Master of Science (M.S.) —Earned after the B.A. or B.S., taking approximately two years of courses in arts or science and writing a thesis.

Doctorates: Philosophy (Ph.D.), Education (Ed.D.)—Usually earned after the Master's degree with advanced, graduate level seminar work and a doctoral thesis based on original research.

Registration Tips

If the school allows, register by mail or phone. This will save you much time. If you must be present at registration, plan to spend a lot of time standing in lines. Be prepared by having all the forms filled out in advance, and a list of alternate courses.

Be sure to have your checkbook or credit card with you. Most schools require payment at registration, although you probably do not have to pay the full amount then. Most schools have payment plans.

Be sure to have your Social Security number with you. These days most schools use your Social Security number as your student identification number.

Don't stay away because you don't have the full tuition at registration. Check with the office for financial aid if you have a financial concern. More about this in a moment.

Don't Wait Until the Last Minute

If you wait until the last minute to enroll, you are likely to find that the class is already full. Once the allotted spaces are gone, no more students will be admitted. That is why it is practical to go to the college a few weeks before registration week to talk with an advisor.

If you want to enroll in a certificate program (usually one year) or in one of the degree programs (from one to three years) talk to an academic adviser at the college *a few months* before starting the program! Here's why:

1. You may need to take special examinations.
2. To enter a degree program you will probably have to obtain a transcript from your high school to show that you graduated and passed all required subjects. (Note: Obtaining a transcript takes time and usually requires a small fee. You may run into delays if you don't send the fee with your request.)
3. You may have to take an English or math placement test. Many entering students do not have the basic skills in math, spelling, grammar, and vocabulary. They need to brush up those skills.

Getting In After a Course is Full

If it is essential that you take a specific course at a certain time of day, but discover that the course is already filled up, don't despair. All schools allow late registration. We suggest doing the following as a possible strategy: Wait until the first class is held, show up and attend the first class. Then, when the class is over, approach the instructor. Tell him or her about your problem. Ask if he or she will grant you permission to attend the course.

Most instructors, when approached in this manner, will allow one more student into the class. This tactic requires some nerve and assertiveness, but it is a way to get into the class of your choice.

Prior Life Experience (PLE) Credits

Some colleges and universities offer PLE (Prior Life Experience) credits. You may receive credit for experiences you have already had. For example: if you have run your own business for ten years and now wish to earn a business degree, PLE credit may be a possibility for you.[1]

Educational institutions offering these credits usually have workshops to help you document your learning. A sizeable amount of writing and validation is required but you may be rich in life experience and able to qualify some of it for official college credit.

Jane, for example, had traveled extensively with her husband (a career military man). She had visited most of the countries in Europe and could speak German fluently. With documented validation of both experiences, she was able to earn college credit in European history, sociology, and foreign language.

Marge wanted to complete a degree in home economics that she had started 25 years previously. She had managed a home, raised three children, and participated in many community improvement committees. She examined the course descriptions required for her major. Life experience fit nicely into some of the courses. She contacted an advisor in the home economics department and verified that PLE could be used toward her degree. She attended a class on documenting her experiences and was able to rapidly complete the home economics requirements for a degree.

Credits must be paid for, but when the push of time and experience is on your side it is an option to consider.

Buy Your Textbooks Early

After you have registered, go to the bookstore and purchase the required textbooks for your courses. The bookstore will have shelves full of textbooks for all the courses. Each shelf will list the instructor and course that the books are for.

Do not wait until after the first class meeting to buy your books because the bookstore may not have ordered enough books for everyone. They generally expect some students to drop the course and bring books back for a refund.

If you buy a used textbook pay close attention to which edition it is. Purchase only the most recent edition of a textbook. Using a used third edition of a textbook when the instructor has switched to the fourth edition will not be acceptable.

When you purchase your textbooks keep your receipts but do

not put your name in your books. If for any reason the course is cancelled or you do not want to stay in it, you can sell your books back to the bookstore for a full refund within a certain time limit.

Locate Your Classrooms

Once you know which classes you will be taking, find the room where each class meets. *Do this before the first day of classes.* When classes start each term, it can be quite hectic fighting through mobs of people to find a place you've never been to! Know where each room is and how you'll get from one place to the next.

Courses Can Be Dropped

If, however, after attending the first one or two classes, you realize you've made a serious mistake, then consider dropping the class or transferring to another course. Remember, though, *it is normal to feel somewhat overwhelmed by a course at first.* Talk to the instructor or check with an advisor before dropping. If you drop a course early, most of your money will be refunded.

How to Get Financial Help

The purpose of financial assistance is to help students who would not be able to attend college without financial help. Financial aid will help in paying the difference between what you can afford to pay and what it will cost you to go to college. All families and individuals are treated equally through the use of a standard way of determining how much you can afford to pay.

This Unmarried Mother on Welfare Succeeded

Late one evening in 1981, 26 year old Carol Sasaki sat with her baby in a bus station. Unmarried and on welfare, she had no money to pay for a room. Her life had been very rough.

She felt that she was bad, abnormal, awful, and that life had passed her by. At that moment a well dressed woman sat down next to Carol and started talking with her. The woman was a college administrator. She said that she had once been on welfare.

The woman encouraged Carol to seek a college education. Carol had dropped out of school when she ran away from home at age 13. She knew she could not read, write, or do arithmetic very well.

Carol came to the college and took some tests. They showed that she was learning disabled. With encouragement, however, she managed to learn basic skills and then pass the high school equivalency test. She obtained public assistance funds to take college courses. She found out about grants and student loans.

She got off welfare. She took as many courses as the college would allow each term. At age 30 she graduated with a B.A. with honors. Carol went on to earn an M.A. and now helps others find ways to finance their education.[2]

Fill Out the Forms

The office for financial aid has information about many sources of money for college students. Be prepared to fill out lots of forms. The forms can appear so overwhelming to the beginning student that some people walk away and never come back. Don't give up! *Many colleges give workshops in how to fill out the forms.* The financial aid personnel will lead you through the forms step-by-step, if necessary.

Many colleges use the FAF (financial aid form) as a way to check eligibility for available scholarships. If you don't qualify this year, be sure to check again. The rules change often. Lack of eligibility one year is not necessarily true the next.

You can get ready to fill out the financial forms by preparing a rough budget of your expenses for the year. Your expenses will include: tuition and fees, books and supplies, room and board, transportation, and personal expenses.

Money is Available in Many Ways

Scholarships are only one form of aid or financial support offered to students. Many programs provide students with grants and loans. Some funds are specifically reserved for OTA students.

A grant is an outright gift, which does not have to be repaid. In some instances, for a person who is without funds, the college may have a way to reduce tuition fees.

Many students qualify for loans at very low interest rates.

Most student loans do not have to be repaid until after graduation. These funds are available from banks, from the federal government, and other sources.

Financial aid can be in the form of reduced tuition. A growing number of senior citizens are taking advantage of the free or reduced costs for people over 62 or 65.

If you are a veteran, you probably know about your GI benefits provided by the federal government; but do you also know that educational benefits may be provided by your state? The office of financial aid can tell you if you qualify.

The U S Department of Education makes funds available to college students through a number of programs:

Pell Grants—up to $2100 for undergraduates enrolled at least half-time; no repayment.

Supplemental Educational Opportunity Grants—up to $4000 a year depending on your need; no repayment.

Guaranteed Student Loans—up to $2,625 the first two years, increase amounts third and fourth years.

Supplemental Loans for Students—up to $4000 each year for students independent of their parents.

Perkins Loans (formerly called National Direct Student Loans)—amount of loan based on financial need and availability of funds. Up to $4500 if enrolled in a vocational program.

Don't Overlook Your Employer

Many employers reimburse employees after a course is successfully completed. If yours has not in the past, it still won't hurt to ask. Special arrangements might be made if you take courses seen as up-grading your skills. You won't know unless you ask.[3]

Another source of funds is through student employment programs. As you will see in the next chapter, there are many jobs available for students who need income.

The main point to keep in mind is that many possibilities exist for helping college students get an education. Don't rule yourself out without checking. Inquire to find out about your eligibility.

Action Review

- [ ] Have I read through the college catalog?
- [ ] Do I have specific courses in mind that I want to take?
- [ ] Have I found out if I need to apply for admission?
- [ ] Have I checked with the financial aid office to find out about my eligibility for financial assistance?
- [ ] Have I inquired about educational benefits or support from my employer?
- [ ] Do I know how to register for the courses I want?
- [ ] Do I know where my classrooms are located?

Success Group Activity

Talk about what difficulties you encountered in trying to get registered for courses. Talk about the courses that you expect to take. Help each other look into ways to tailor your selection of courses to fit your unique interests and needs. Be frank with each other about your financial needs. Someone in your group may know of a way to get extra financial help.

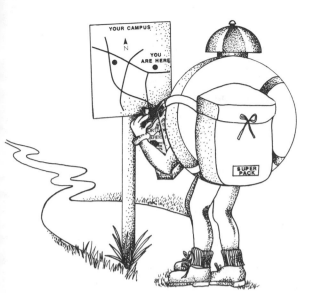

Chapter 4

Orientation: Getting Acquainted with Your Campus

Could you tell another student about all the free services available to you?

Do you know what recreation facilities are available to you?

Do you know where the health service is?

Have you found out about transportation services?

Do you know where to go with questions about class schedules?

Be Assertive About Orientation

Your college tries to inform you of every facility and service available to you. Regardless of how hard the orientation leaders try, they are bound to overlook something. This chapter describes the college support services and facilities you should know about. You can use this chapter as your checklist. As you go through whatever form of orientation your college offers, become familiar with all the services and facilities we list that are offered by your college.

If you have completed an orientation program, use this chapter to review your knowledge of campus services. Orientation is a continuous process throughout your time in college. You will need the various resources at one time or another. Make sure you know what they offer and where they are located.

If possible, pay a visit to every service or facility to check it out. For example, most colleges have learning skills centers and writing improvement centers. Often, to find out about what these support services can offer you, you'll need to stop in and have a chat with a staff member. *Don't hesitate.* You'll usually find that staff members of college support services are trying to think up ways to insure that students make use of their services.

Take the Tour

Most colleges provide guided tours during the orientation program. In addition, you'll probably be provided with loads of information about the program, facilities, and opportunities available. The information given to you will probably contain a "survival kit." The packet should describe various services and facilities available to you.

If you look around campus, you will find free copies of the college newspaper. The first edition of the new school year will probably be a special orientation edition to acquaint new students with the various activities on campus.

The more quickly you become familiar with your campus, the more you will feel at home. Learn why certain offices and facilities exist, even if you don't use them now. At some point it may be to your advantage to know where and why most offices and services exist.

College Services Checklist

Academic Advising

Academic advisors are available to provide information on class schedules, course requirements for specific majors, eligibility for certain programs, and such. Peer advisors, specially trained students, may meet with you to help with course selection.

Activity Center or Student Union

The student center is the heart of student activity. You may find cafeterias, art displays, television rooms, reading rooms, possibly a bowling alley, a barber shop, ping-pong tables, and pool tables. The student center on every campus is unique, so take time to familiarize yourself with this building. On the bulletin boards you will find announcements for various student activities such as theater offerings and college film offerings.

☆ TIP: Find out if lockers are available for rent. A locker at school is a great place to leave heavy books, keep your lunch, store an extra umbrella, and serve as a place where friends can leave notes for you!

Admissions/Orientation/Office for Re-entry Students

On larger campuses these will probably be separate offices. On smaller campuses they may be combined. In any case, these are the offices with people who know the answers to your questions or who know how to get the answers. The people in these offices are hired to help students with questions.

Bookstore

Take some time to go through the bookstore. Browse around to see where supplies and different books are located. The front part of the store usually contains *trade* books. These are books available to the general public and are sold in almost all college bookstores. At the back of the store you will probably find a textbook section. Books will be arranged on shelves listed by course numbers within the different departments of the college.

Campus Security

Find out how to get help from campus security in case of an emergency. They are the people to call first when any sort of help from police is needed. Make friends with the security officers. They appreciate it. They may help with minor car problems or contact your family if you have an emergency.

Cashier's Office

All monetary matters involving tuition are handled here. Be sure to inquire about any available payment plans. The cashier's office will probably cash checks for any person with a valid student body ID card.

Center for Adult Students

Many schools now have a designated area where the older students, sometimes called *re-entry* students, can go for information about problems or concerns.

Counseling Center/Career Counseling

In these centers professional counselors are available for private sessions with students who want to talk about personal concerns. If you run into problems with instructors or other school personnel, counselors can serve as your advocate. Career counselors usually have access to an array of instruments/materials designed to help students clarify their career goals. These centers usually have books, cassette tapes, and other materials you can use or borrow.

Day-Care Center

If you have preschool children, the college may provide day care. You can bring children to school with you and for a low fee have the child cared for and fed by professionals while you are in school.

Dean of Students

This is the office to contact if you have any questions or difficulties that are not immediately handled some place else. The dean of students is responsible for seeing that you are well taken care of in school and that any problems you have can be solved.

Dean of Instruction

This is an important office on every campus. Here you will find help with academic questions and problems such as: changing a mistake in your transcript of grades, removing an incomplete in a course, getting permission to take more than the allowed number of course hours, waiving a course requirement, getting into a course already filled, or arranging for special academic programs.

Handicapped Student Services

Special assistance will be available to help handicapped students succeed. Such assistance may include notetakers, readers, writers, or sign language interpreters. The assistance counselors will have many practical suggestions. They can also help students obtain adaptive equipment, transportation, and other services from your state's vocational rehabilitation department.

Health Service

Every campus has a medical help available for emergency medical care and treatment. The health service may be a resource for information, programs, and services on alcohol and drug abuse, birth control, blood pressure testing, cholesterol screening, and so forth. Costs are usually included in fees or are very low. Inquire, if you wish, about student health insurance. Rates are very low and it can cover family members.

Learning Center

Many schools have special centers where you go to learn a specific subject. You tell the person in charge what you want. You will then be assigned to a booth with a set of earphones, a television monitor, or a computer terminal. You work at your own speed at the lesson you are there to complete. You can stay with it as long as you wish. Don't feel intimidated, the person in charge will be glad to explain how everything works.

Library

Visit the library and take some time to walk through it. You can go almost any place in the library to see what is available. You will notice that in a college library there are many desks, tables, and study areas. Librarians usually enjoy telling people about library services. Take advantage of their helpfulness.

Most libraries have typing rooms, video viewing rooms, conference areas, and quiet rooms for listening to music. For rest and relaxation (R&R) or research this is one resource you shouldn't overlook.

Registrar

The registrar's office is responsible for keeping all academic records. If you have earned college credit elsewhere the registrar's office can give you information on how to claim credit and obtain documentation so that it will apply to your program. After you graduate, the registrar's office provides transcripts that may be requested at future times.

Sports Center

As a student, you should have access at certain times to the sports facilities. Take your time to inquire, because having a nice swim between classes might be exactly the right thing for you. There will be an exercise room that you can use when available. There may be a track for jogging, and other possibilities for exercise. You may be able to check out equipment free of charge.

> I found that during certain hours I could use the workout rooms used by the athletes! I could use the track and courts even if I wasn't taking a physical education class. And for a small fee I could occasionally take one of my daughters swimming. —MK

Student Activities Office

Every college has a number of student-run organizations. The student body president, other officers, and many student project coordinators are located in the student activities office.

Student Employment Office

A separate office may exist to coordinate job offers from local employers with students who are looking for off-campus work. There are many jobs in every community that fit perfectly with being a student. This office will provide assistance with résumé writing and interviewing skills. They will help you find employment upon graduation.

Student Housing

Your school may provide student housing in its own residence halls. It may also coordinate placement of students into private homes and facilities that exist in the nearby area. Local landlords may register the availability of housing with this office. Larger colleges will have housing for married students and their families.

Study Skills Center

This center is staffed with specialists on teaching people how to read faster, remember better, pass tests more easily, and, in general, to succeed in the academic aspects of school. Improving study skills often is the solution to dealing with emotional problems.

Transportation Office

If you have to commute to school you may need a permit to park in the campus parking lots. Inquire about car pools or buses as an alternative to driving your own car each day.

Explore Your College

Take time now to get acquainted with your school. Be active and curious, not passive or timid. Learn about the many resources available to you. You will feel comfortable coming to campus more quickly, and the more that you locate and use resources, the more successful you will be.

☆ REMEMBER: *The entire school exists to help you get the education you want!*

Action Review

☐ Have I explored the campus to find out what is available to students?

☐ Do I know where the health service is?

☐ Do I know how to reach campus security?

☐ Do I know where to inquire about transportation, day care, career counseling, and other services?

☐ Have I familiarized myself with the activities center?

☐ Do I feel well oriented to the college?

Success Group Activity

Plan a resources treasure hunt. Make up a list of places, offices, centers, and services that want to know about. Be sure to include the nearby neighborhood in your exploration. Find the location of stores, bank branches, the post office, copy centers, eating places, book stores, and yogurt shops. Split up into search teams. Divide up the list. Agree to meet at a certain place at a certain time. Afterwards talk with each other about what you found.

Chapter 5

Your Family: How to Gain Their Support and Encouragement

Do you feel guilty about doing something just for yourself?

Can you ask people for help when you need it?

Do you wonder if you will upset your family because you are going to school?

Do you know how to develop and follow a positive plan of action for getting the help and support you need?

Do you understand what it means to give your family high-quality time?

There's a Way, If You Will...

Your family does not have to feel deprived by the extra time you spend in school. If mealtime conversation is filled with interesting conversational tidbits, if dreams of an exciting tomorrow are shared with those who are close, and they see a happier, more enthusiastic person, they will be glad for you.[1]

You Can Make It Work

Making the pieces fit, maintaining relationships and school successfully takes time and planning. You will not find all the adjustments or solutions over-night. Fitting into a new role is never easy and it may take six months to a year before you and those close to you have made the transition.

Getting an education is the best insurance you can buy for a successful, secure future. Learning is a lifelong experience. Finding the right combination for relationships, work, and school can pay off big dividends in personal and professional satisfaction.

How to Gain the Support You Need

Here is a simple, but effective way to get support, help, encouragement, and understanding from your family and friends:

1. Take some time privately to think about the support you need from others in your new role as a student.
2. Decide to seek that support.
3. Talk to the people whose support you are seeking. Explain why going to school is important to you. Ask what worries they might have and listen with understanding. Ask what positive feelings they have about your going back to school and what advantages they may see for themselves.
4. Be very specific in asking for the support you need—undisturbed time alone, encouragement, household chores done, etc.
5. Track positives with people. Reward any actions you regard as positive, helpful, or supportive with thanks and appreciation. Give others immediate feedback about what you like.

Plan ahead

Think through what you want to talk about and what requests you will make. Select the best time to talk.

Taking night classes may mean that the family mealtime will be disrupted. If you are working full time and going to school part time, you will have less time together. Find out how they feel about this change and empathize with their concerns rather than telling them not to feel the way they do. Let them know that your time together is important to you.

If people are reluctant to talk about what is ahead, make some effort to get them to think about the months and years ahead. It is essential to keep the lines of communication open to avoid a big blowup someday at just the wrong time.

Don't assume the worst, however, you may be surprised!

> Before I started to school I sat down with the three teenage children who were still at home and talked with them about what changes might occur in their lives as a result of my commitment to school. The kids were wonderful! They encouraged me so heartily I should have been suspicious, but I wasn't....Years later, after they were out of high school, they told me they were eager to get me involved elsewhere so that they would have more freedom to come and go as they wanted! —MK

Let People Know What You Want

Students with families have requests such as these:

I would like my three teenage children to do more housework, so that I would have more time for my studies.

I'd like my husband and kids to fix dinner for themselves a couple of nights a week when I am at class.

It would be nice to have my wife ask me about my courses and spend a little time talking about my experiences as a student.

I'd appreciate being left alone to study three nights a week; that means not knocking on my door or interrupting to tell me about something on TV.

Why don't people get what they want? The answer is surprising. They usually have not asked.

Most of us were raised not to be selfish. Some selfishness is essential, however, when expressed in a way that is not demanding.

Most people report that once they have the courage to ask for support, they receive far more than they expected. Some students report that when they finally ask for what they want, the reply is "Why didn't you ask before? Sure, I'll be glad to do that!"

Getting Help at Home

Those in a home management career know there are certain maintenance tasks that must be done—homework, or not. When dirty socks and underwear carpet the floor, it is time for some cooperation and delegation. Most children over the age of seven, and most partners, can learn to pick up, sort, and put the clothes in the washing machine.

Even a four-year-old can help fold clothes and put them away. To paraphrase, "Ask not what you can do for your children, but what can they do for you!" As roles change, it is time to delegate responsibilities to others in the family.

Have a meeting with the family each week to develop a chore schedule. On a piece of paper, list the jobs each person agrees to do and specify when it will be done. It helps to assign the responsibility for developing the weekly list to one of the older children. Participate in the discussion, of course, but when you have one of the older children write down the various duties and place the list in a conspicuous place, it will seem less imposed by you.

Post your own weekly time schedule in a conspicuous place so that all can see where you will be and when. When members of your family see that Thursday evening from 7:30 to 9:00 is a study period, they will be more likely to leave you alone, *especially if you stick with your own schedule!*

☆ TIP: Children will be less likely to interrupt or intrude during your study hours if you set aside specific times during the week for each one.

Quality is Better Than Quantity

Reserve one solid hour each week for each child. Children will be less demanding when they know that they have their own special time with you. Talk with Cheryl about when she'd like her hour. Write "Cheryl's hour" in big letters on your schedule. Then make sure she gets her hour to be with you. Do not try to fit more than one child into the same hour. Make these hours very important to you. Avoid missing one or changing one if you possibly can.

Let the child decide what will be done during the hour. Children's self-esteem develops by being in close contact with their parents, by being seen as unique, and by being able to influence their world. So don't plan this hour; let the child influence what you do together. Be curious about what develops. Many parents who have done this report that their relationships and contact with their children have significantly improved.

Working together on tasks at home can be important time together. As one sets the table, another scrubs the potatoes, someone unloads the dishwasher, and the microwave zaps the main course, each person talks about their day. Time for sharing is essential when you have to juggle work, home, and school. Sharing, caring, and doing the work together can all be done at the same time.

Use A Little Psychology

Thousands of experiments conducted by psychologists over the years have established the validity of a principle that affects the actions of others. The principle is:

☆ *Actions that are rewarded tend to increase.*

Consequently,

1. If you thank, compliment, and reward others for doing what is helpful to you they will do even more.
2. If you stop rewarding, they'll do less of what is helpful.

What rewards can you use? Here is a list of suggestions from adult students about things they've done:

- Express appreciation.
- Say "thank you."
- Buy or fix their favorite food for them.
- Give hugs and kisses.
- Give treats or little gifts.
- Be interested in their lives.
- Tell them about something interesting at school.
- Speak highly of them to others.
- Give them back rubs and neck massages.
- Let them feel that your success is their success.
- Ask what they would like from you.
- Leave nice notes for them; send cards.

When you speak clearly about what you would like from others and then follow up with rewards, you usually get results that exceed your expectations. Most families respond in very positive ways. In fact, you may be overwhelmed by the tremendous love and support your family shows you.

Expect Surprises

Expect some surprises and be prepared to make some adjustments of your own when your family changes. Letting people do things their own way may be difficult at first, but a positive attitude and a sense of humor can pull you through.

In one family, for example, the children (grade-school age) volunteered to cook dinner one evening a week. They accepted full responsibility for shopping, cooking, and cleaning up afterward. Their mother said she assumed the meal would be done the way she always did it. She reported:

> The first time they "cooked" dinner they met me at the door all excited and led me to the dining room before I could take off my coat. I expected steaming plates with vegetables, salad, and so forth. When I walked in my eyes almost fell out of my head. Their idea of a great dinner was boiled hot dogs served on paper plates with a bottle of pop, a bag of potato chips, and Twinkies for dessert! I didn't know whether to collapse in hysterical laughter or lecture them on the right way to shop, cook, and serve a

nutritious meal. I did neither. As I sat there eating a barely warm wiener, I told myself it wouldn't kill me to let them do it their way. I've had some interesting meals since then. Peanut butter sandwiches and pie aren't too bad. And the paper plates are real time and energy savers.

Things Don't Always Work Out

Some students find that their home situations do not get better. Some family members may become difficult. A husband may start to drink more or stay out late. Children may begin to get into trouble or have difficulty at school.

If anything this extreme takes place, it is important to seek professional advice and counseling. Get to know what services are available at the college. There are many experts you can talk to and a variety of sources of help. Other students can provide support and practical advice. Ask around and you are likely to discover that more good solutions are possible than you imagined.

They Need Emotional Support

It can be easy to forget that family and friends need some nurturing, too. An instructor once said to an over-achieving beginner, "When it comes to a choice of studying extra to get an A on the mid-term (working overtime) or taking your children to the zoo—take the kids to the zoo." A little attention in time saves resentment in the long run.

When you return to school, people close to you may react as though you are changing the rules on them. A change in your daily routines forces them to change theirs, and they may resist.

Adult students find the return easier if they are prepared for the mixed emotions that others may have about their changed roles. It helps to understand their feelings, and then help them see that your going back to school is good for them as well.

Bev had four children when she decided to return to school. Two seemed to adjust fine to the new schedule, but one daughter was getting more "mouthy" and her son said resentfully, "Why can't you be like other mommies and just stay home?"

The next term Bev scheduled classes so she could be at home when the children came home from school. She started a ten-minute contact time for each child where sharing the day and hugging and touching was made a priority when they first came home. The discipline and resentment problems disappeared.

It May Take a While

The more your family has been dependent on you, the more difficult it will be for them to be more responsible for themselves. If the family resists, making the change can be difficult. They may become upset and refuse to talk. They may accuse you of being selfish and of not caring about them.

There are many reasons for such reactions. A husband may secretly fear that if his wife becomes capable, educated, and employable, she may decide to leave. A wife may not like having her husband work full time and then devote evenings and weekends to school. She feels neglected.

The key, as with most challenges in life, is to not let them make you feel guilty, but to look with understanding at the other person's feelings. Look to see what is legitimate about what they feel but don't take too much responsibility for their feelings. Would you let your ten-year-old control how you drive or where you go? Are your children better qualified to make decisions about your life than you are? Does your partner know your needs better than you do?

Hold true to your plan for yourself while you give your family time to adjust to this new way of life. Let them know how important they are to you.

Develop a Plan and Be Positive

Going to school can solve problems. Try to use your returning to school as an opportunity to improve your relationship with your loved ones. Healthy relationships are based on people supporting each other's growth and development, not dependence. Your returning to school could lead to deeper, closer, and warmer feelings of love and appreciation than you ever thought possible.

George was feeling out of touch with his wife, Kathy. They both worked and went to school. It seemed they never talked anymore.

Together they looked at both of their schedules. They made Wednesday lunch and Sunday morning brunch dates as top priorities. George says now "I'd never think of missing one of these dates. That is the time we still know we are in tune with each other and share our triumphs and frustrations. We are back to being best friends."

Include Them

Make them feel included in your world, not excluded. Try to create the feeling "We are going to college." If your instructor will allow a visit, and if appropriate, consider taking a family member to a class.

The more they know about what you do, the more they can understand and support you. A Saturday tour around campus can help introduce them to your new world. Take your spouse or older children to athletic events or concerts. Find out if they can use the PE facilities. Bring them to the library with you some evening.

Going back to school can be the best gift you give your school-age children. As they study, you study. The message comes through loud and clear; education is a priority in this family. Gathering together to do your homework can be much more bonding for a family than "zoning out" in front of the TV.

Also, when your children know you struggle with school, it gets you off the parental pedestal and on a level leading to better understanding. If your child can help you learn math, so much the better. If they can help demystify the world of computers, you both benefit!

Family and friends need to know they are still a priority in your life. Give them good quality time. Time will be treasured more as the demands of school increase. TV and for fun reading may bite the dust, but good personal relationships are an essential success foundation as you juggle work, home, and school.

Action Review: Checklist of Useful Actions

☐ Have I talked with others about returning to school and how this will affect our lives?

☐ Have I listened well to the concerns of others?

☐ Have I asked for support in a direct, clear, and specific way?

☐ Can I ask for what I need without feeling guilty or demanding?

☐ Do I tell people often enough how much I appreciate their efforts to help?

☐ Do I have a variety of reinforcements available that I can use to express appreciation?

☐ Have I acquainted myself with all the professional resources available to me at school in case I need advice?

☐ Do I have an active, positive plan to make things work out?

Success Group Activity

Talk with each other about what you have done to enlist the support of your family. Discuss how it feels to make selfish requests. Help each other problem solve specific challenges. Compliment each other for progress you have made. Be sure to tell each other about amusing incidents and your successes.

Chapter 6

How to Balance Going to College with Working

Do you know that over 50% of all two-year college students work part or full time?

Do you know that part-time college students account for the greatest increase in college population?

Do you know that most careers will require you to be a life-long learner?

Do you know that you can earn college credit by combining work and school?

Scheduling Work and School

Colleges have responded to the needs of students who work. The times and places you take your college work are becoming more flexible. Evening and weekend courses are available. All-day workshops add options.

If your working hours are flexible you may be able to schedule your courses on Mondays, Wednesdays, and Fridays only, or just mornings or afternoons to accommodate your job.

Keep in mind that you do not have to take all of your courses from the same college. If a course at a different college fits your schedule better you may be able to take that course and transfer the credit. Transferring credit is easy to do between state-supported colleges.

Course-Load Guidelines

If you work full time, you probably should take no more than two classes in college at one time. The rule of thumb: for every hour of class time, you need two or three hours to do the homework for that class. Thus, if you spend six hours a week in class, you will spend 12 to 18 hours a week in preparation. Add that to a 40-hour work week and you have a sizeable commitment. Travel time from work to school and back to home must also be considered.

If you are going to school full time, work outside school should be kept to 20 hours, or fewer. When you work over 20 hours, your work, or school, or both, are likely to suffer from the overload.

A few students choose jobs that pay less if studying is possible at times on the job. Some students know they need the physical release of a lot of activity after classes and deliberately choose a job involving physical labor.

Work-study jobs can allow split-shift work around class schedules. For some, splitting up school and work is helpful; for others, it is fragmenting There is no right or wrong way to combine work and school but there is a way that works best for you. The challenge is to find it.

Employers Will Help You

Employers need educated workers. They need people who can learn fast, people who can learn new technology and new skills, people who can adapt to a rapidly changing world.

In recent years employers have created many ways to encourage, support, and pay for the education of the workers they need. It is estimated that industry now spends from $40 to $60 billion on educational training each year. Employers work closely with colleges to offer a variety of ways to blend working with your college education.

Merging Learning and Work

Most colleges now offer programs for getting college credit for work experience. Credit is offered in a variety of ways that include cooperative education, work-study programs, internships, and practicums,

Cooperative Work Experience

Cooperative work experience allows a student to work and earn college credit while exploring a career choice. When a student has chosen a major such as business, computer science, or engineering the school's cooperative education department can help arrange work experience in the field.[1]

A student may have a particular job site in mind, or the cooperative work specialist may find an appropriate work placement in the student's major field of study. Specific learning experiences are defined and the student is supervised in meeting the objectives. The average co-op student earns $7,000 per year, although some placements are arranged on a volunteer basis.

Cooperative education personnel maintain close contact with companies designated as co-op sites. Everything is done to ensure a good learning experience.

It is not possible to receive retroactive credit in co-op, but it is possible to earn college credit for present employment. If your present work is within the field of your college major, or you are doing certain kinds of work to see if you wish to make it your major field of study, it is worth contacting your cooperative education department to look into the possibility of receiving college credit for your present job.[2]

Work Study

Colleges hire many students to work on campus. The federal government provides funds for the college work-study program. Work-study students must qualify for their jobs by showing financial need.

Student-help jobs are also available. They require only that the student is competent to do the work .

Those in the work-study and student-help programs fill in at libraries, locker rooms, receptionists' desks, laboratories, cafeterias, counseling offices, school grounds, and many other college locations. Usually, they work for the minimum wage but the work experience can be valuable training. It can help clarify career goals and be included on a résumé. These jobs often allow you some study time on the job and your supervisor shifts your work hours to fit your class schedule and exam times.

Everyone Benefits

If you haven't had much paid work experience, a work-study job can be a good confidence builder. It is a way to prove your worth in the work world. There is a tendency for more organizations to offer positions for students. They recognize that involving students in work experience is a good way to screen potential employees. It also helps the work-study student to build job contacts. Your financial aid office has information about these opportunities.

Joan, a single parent struggling to get off welfare, started working for the counseling department in a clerical capacity as a work-study student. Her work and life experience helped solidify her choice of social work as a college major. The department was able to set up a co-op work experience to help her earn college credits.

Later, when Joan needed a practicum site for her degree, the counseling department set up an information referral position in job placement. When she was granted her degree in social work, Joan had incorporated enough practical, professional experience to have a decided edge on other graduates. Valuable contacts and recommendations were hers—and securing a job, using her new credentials, was no problem.

Internship Programs

An internship is a training position that usually pays you for acquiring a skill. Internships may be offered where expensive equipment or the need for highly trained professionals make on-the-job training cost effective. Prerequisite skills are taught in the classroom, but most of the new learning takes place in the work place.

Two vocational career fields that use internships extensively are electronic engineering technician and radio/TV broadcasting. These industries grow and change so rapidly that few colleges have the funds or facilities for the latest equipment and cannot meet salary scales to hire top people in these fields.

A partnership is formed where education experts break the learning process into manageable steps, write the curriculum, assign credit, provide on-site consultation, and see that complementary classwork is provided. Internship programs often lead to a two-year associate degree.

Practicum Training Experiences

Practicum experiences differ from internships in that they often require a year or more of classroom work before a student is allowed on-the-job practical experience. Para-professional programs (teacher assistant, legal assistant, alcohol/drug counselor) have significant practical experience as an essential part of their vocational degree program.

Anywhere from three months to over a year may be involved in this on-the-job training and experience. This practicum training is coupled with classroom discussion and job supervision. The students rarely receive payment for practicum experience but college credit is earned.

Balancing Different Work Demands

Many jobs have peak demand periods. In school, it's mid-terms and finals. In retail sales, pre-Christmas shopping will keep you hopping. For colleges, fall registration is a busy time for support services. If you have school-age children summer vacation can be extra demanding.

When work times are predictably busy, lighten your school load to accommodate busy times. Get that paper in early; move ahead in your reading; talk with your teacher to get a jump on early work—or an approved delay, if needed.

For those who juggle work and school, knowing about and using your options is a survival tool. Trying to cram full-time work, full-time school, and demanding personal relationships into twenty-four hours can lead a person to early burn-out. It is not how fast you can get there, but rather, are you enjoying the process? Can you go the distance? That's what counts!

Bread and Butter Jobs (That don't interfere with academic success)

If you need a "bread and butter" job to help with expenses while you go to school, don't expect it to be the delight of your dreams. You can, however, make it work with your school schedule. It would be a bonus if it were somehow related to your career choice, but it does not have to be connected. What is essential is that you can earn a certain amount of money to take care of the "bread and butter" of survival.

How do you nail down such a job? The same rules apply here that you use searching for career employment. In a nut shell:

- Know what skills and personal qualities you have to offer.
- Let everyone know you are looking for a job.
- Be prepared to state your case with enthusiasm.
- Practice common job interview questions and answers.
- Make contacts at best hours and days, Tuesday-Thursday, 10 a.m.-11 a.m. and 2 p.m.-3 p.m.
- Dress for success, be clean, careful, conservative, classic.

- Let your attitude show you really want the job.
- You "make it or break it" in the first three minutes of the interview.
- Keep employer's needs in mind.
- Have accurate information ready for job application.
- Tell them the best time of day to contact you and what phone number to call.
- Send a thank-you note for the interview.
- Before accepting a job consider the location. Is it close to campus or will commuting be a problem?
- Be alert to opportunities. A "bread and butter" job can lead to a "caviar and champagne" career!

You Can Successfully Combine Work With School

We hope that this information has expanded your thinking about what is available for college students in the way of employment these days. Look around. Talk with people. It is quite possible that you can find a work situation that fits your schedule and your educational program while providing you with much needed income.

Action Review

Check the following list for balancing work and school:

❑ Do I make realistic school and work demands on myself?

❑ Have I explored the posibility of getting college credit for work experience?

❑ Have I asked my employer about ways that my educational efforts could be paid for or reimbursed?

❑ Have I looked at new developments and changes in the job market?

❑ Have I combined employment with career development opportunities?

Success Group Activity

Do the members of your group work? What sort of balance between work and study have you each arranged? What do you know about ways to work for pay, earn college credit, and gain on-the-job experience?

Chapter 7

Why Some Students Are More Successful than Others

Can you describe the differences between successful and unsuccessful students?

Do you know what it means to view college as a learning environment?

Do you know how to take good lecture notes?

Are your educational and career goals self-chosen?

Successful Students...

Success in college is not determined by your IQ. Success comes from acting in ways that result in you succeeding in your courses. Counselors and others who work with college students know quite well why some students are more successful than others. Successful students:

- find out at the first class meeting when all the tests will be held and when papers or projects are due
- attend all classes
- sit up front
- prepare for each class in advance
- ask intelligent questions during class
- take good lecture notes
- organize their time with a personal schedule
- study regularly
- set specific study goals each time they study
- prepare for tests by writing practice tests
- stop studying when they have accomplished their study goals

In addition to the actions listed above, successful students:

- feel motivated by personal goals
- know that how well they do in college and in life is their responsibility

Accept Responsibility for Learning

College is a learning environment, it is not a teaching environment. Your instructors are responsible only for presenting ideas and information to you. In college the responsibility is on the learner, not on the teacher.

You cannot passively sit back and expect instructors to entertain you. It is not the instructor's responsibility to draw you into learning or to make sure you get your assignments done, the way it was in high school. Succeeding in college is your responsibility.

Find Out What is Required

Successful students actively determine the requirements for each course. During the first lecture, find out answers to these key questions:

Which chapters in the textbook will be covered?
When will the exams be given?
What material will each exam cover?
What type of questions will be on the exams—essay, multiple choice?
Will other work be required?
When will the work be due?
How will grading in the course be determined?
Does the instructor have an outline of the most important terms and concepts to be covered?

These questions are a starting point. Others will occur as you go along.

☆ A WORD OF CAUTION: Don't make instructors feel that they are being cross-examined. Be assertive, but *tactful*.

In general, you will find that instructors enjoy answering questions about their courses. A few instructors may be poorly prepared, however, and could become defensive if pressed too hard.

Some instructors will have written handouts. If you don't receive a handout, be sure to write everything down in your notebook.

Take Good Lecture Notes

Writing down what the instructor says in lectures is active listening. You are also being realistic about the nature of human memory. Human beings quickly forget most of what they hear no matter how much they would like to be able to remember.

Several days after hearing a lecture, the best that most students can do is to recall about ten percent of what was said. So, unless you tape record the lectures or alternate note taking with a friend, you need to take notes at every lecture.

Unsuccessful students don't take notes. If you ask a student who doesn't take notes to fill you in on something the instructor said last week, you will quickly learn for yourself how important note taking is for accurate remembering.

Lectures are like textbook chapters. Each usually has a main theme and makes several important points. If you listen for them, they will be easier to hear.

We encourage you to take lecture notes in outline form. This habit will help you to focus on the main points that can be turned into questions. Your job is to record these questions and to make sure that you know how your instructor would answer them.

Tips About Taking Notes

Use a separate notebook for each course. Be sure to write your name, address, and phone number in each notebook.

Do not place notes from different courses on the same pages or in the same notebook. Date each day's notes.

Use an outline form whenever possible. The most commonly used outline form is this:

I. (roman numerals for major topics)
    A. (capital letters for major subgroups)
        1. (numbers for supporting examples, people, points)
        2.
    B.
        1.
            a. (small letters for supporting details)
            b.
            c.
        2.
        3.

Guidelines for Taking Notes

1. During the lecture, take notes on the right-hand side of the paper. Leave a margin on the left.

2. Write down complete phrases and statements, rather than single words.
3. Underline points the instructor gives special emphasis to.
4. After the lecture, take several minutes to complete sentences and fill in material you didn't have time to write. Then turn your outline into test questions. Each lecture will usually supply you with five to seven good exam questions. Write them in the left-hand margin.
5. Leave the back of each page blank. Use it later for taking study notes and writing questions from other sources such as your textbook or assigned reading.

This procedure will help you organize what your instructors present in lectures. Go to lectures looking for questions and their answers. If you come out of each lecture with several questions and answers, you'll be pleased. They are likely to be on your next test!

Sample Notes

Your notes may not look as neat as those below. We don't expect you to carry a typewriter to class. If your notes are neat and as close to outlined as possible, you'll have a much better chance of turning them into a good set of questions. These notes were taken at an introductory psychology lecture. The topic was learning.

LEARNING - November 17

I. Behavior Modification—B.F. Skinner
     (worked with pigeons)
     A. Focus on spontaneous behaviors
          1. Experimenter must wait for behavior to occur
          2. Linked to somatic nervous system
     B. Main principles:
          1. Behaviors reinforced tend to increase
               (Note: Term is *reinforcement*, not *reward*)
          2. Behaviors ignored tend to decrease
          3. Behaviors punished may be temporarily

suppressed but may increase, punishment
can be reinforcing!
C. Tracking positives plan:
1. Specify the desired observable behavior.
2. Choose a reinforcer (that works).
3. Measure current level of desired behavior.
4. Watch for slightest increase in the desired
behavior.
5. Give reinforcer (quick as possible).
II. Classical Conditioning—Ivan Pavlov
(observed dogs salivating when bell rang)...

From notes such as these it is easy to develop practice questions that come very close to what the instructor will ask.

Motivate Yourself with Self-Chosen Personal Goals

Success is to reach a goal. Successful students are students who choose and achieve their goals. Reaching any goal that you selected and worked for makes you successful.

The key is to make certain that your goals are self-chosen. It is less satisfying and less motivating to try to accomplish goals that other people have given you.

Self-chosen goals are motivating. Once you establish personal goals you want to accomplish, your goals give you direction. A personal goal that is useful for you:

1. fits you well; it enables you to mesh your interests, personality, skills, and values
2. excites you; you can hardly wait to get started
3. is definite and specific; you know exactly what it is you're aiming for
4. is measurable; you will be able to see and evaluate your progress
5. is challenging; it isn't easy to reach; it's a good test for you, but achievable
6. will be personally satisfying to reach

If you do not have specific career goals or personal life goals, read through Appendix A at the back of this book. Talk with counselors in the careers center at your college. There is a wealth of helpful information available to you. Remember, be an *active* learner!

> I got top grades. Mostly, it was because I attended all classes, and generally put a lot of time and effort into learning. However, I also made sure that every teacher knew my name by the end of the quarter. My usual technique was to sit in the front of the room, and to ask one intelligent question during every class or two early in the quarter (the sort of question developed only by studying the class material outside of class). Once I felt that the professor recognized me as a student that cared about the material covered in the class, I made an appointment during office hours and pursued some other aspect of the course material with the professor. In this way, I was able to get the person to add a name to the face of the inquisitive and interested older student who sat in the front row. I'm sure that where my grade was borderline a couple of times, I was given the advantage because of the reputation I so carefully cultivated for myself. It couldn't have hurt.—MK

Develop Good Study Habits

Successful students learn good study habits. Your habits determine whether or not you learn much during the time you spend studying. Two students may spend exactly the same amount of time in classes and studying, but the student with good study habits learns more and gets a better education than the student with poor study habits. The chapters ahead will describe good study habits and show how you can develop them.

Action Review: Checklist for Success

☐ Do I act in ways that lead to success in college?

- [ ] Do I take good lecture notes?

- [ ] Do I take time immediately after class to fill in details and indicate key ideas that will probably be questions on exams?

- [ ] Have I accepted responsibility for being a learner?

- [ ] Do I have career or personal life goals that excite me and motivate me?

- [ ] Would I like to change any habits and, if so, am I willing to make the effort?

Success Group Activity

Together, as a group, make up a your own list describing what students do that makes them successful. To provide contrast, make up a second list of what students do that reduces their chance of succeeding. Include what attitudes and habits you believe help or hinder success in college.

To have even more fun with this, each of you arrange to interview several students that you see being very successful. Find out what they say about why they are successful. Get back together and report what you learned. Then write up a summary what you learned so that you can each have a copy. (Note: We'd like to see what you come up with. Please send a copy to us at the address at the end of the book. Thanks.)

Chapter 8

How to Manage Your Time and Study Efficiently

Do you know how to create monthly and weekly schedules?

Are you both a self-starter and a self-stopper?

Do you know how to set study goals?

Do you know that learning is speeded up and study time decreased by outlining the tasks necessary to reach your goals?

Do you know why daily "to do" lists are helpful?

Can you work on high-priority items while ignoring less important matters?

Start With Goals

Study goals help you focus your time and energy. They help you take the step-by-step actions that lead to reaching your dream for a better future. Setting goals is one of the best ways to motivate yourself to study efficiently and effectively.

Students who don't set goals or schedule their time are usually uncertain about what to do from hour to hour. When you identify what you should study to pass a course, and set up a schedule to achieve your study goals, you'll be in good shape. Here's how to set study goals and design a schedule to achieve your goals.

Determine What Your Study Goals Should Be

First, you have to ask, "What do I have to do to pass the course?" In most courses you have to do the following:

1. Pass tests.
2. Pass quizzes.
3. Write papers.
4. Participate in class discussions.
5. Complete projects.

Next, ask these questions when setting up a study schedule:

1. When is each test, paper, or project due?
2. How can I space my studying so that I don't put everything off until the end?
3. How much should I do each day if I wish to accomplish everything on schedule?

After answering these questions, you'll be better equipped to design an effective schedule for completing study goals. You will know where you are going, how you will get there, and how to know when you can stop!

How to Manage Your Time

Fill in Your Calendar

Your greatest aid will be a time schedule. Start by purchasing a calendar with spaces that you can fill in with important dates and obligations. Obtain a big year-at-a-glance calendar or a monthly calendar that you can tear apart and pin up on your wall. You want to be able to see what is ahead for the entire term or semester.

Fill in dates when examinations will take place, when papers and projects are due. Next, fill in all the times that you plan to go to concerts, shows, family gatherings, meetings or other events.

Create Weekly Schedules

After developing a picture of your major commitments for the months ahead, you are now ready to make up a weekly schedule of your classes, study hours, and other obligations. A weekly schedule gives you a clear picture of what you are doing with your time. It helps you spot an extra hour or two during the day that you can use for studying or other activities. A schedule helps you plan more free time to do what you want. It decreases the amount of time you waste.[1]

Follow these steps for effective scheduling:

1. Establish a well-defined and reasonable schedule.
2. Budget time to prepare for each class and all examinations.
3. Budget time to take care of personal responsibilities.
4. Plan to study course notes as soon as possible after each class period.
5. Give difficult subjects preferred times with the fewest possible interruptions and disturbances.
6. Reserve time for your family and leisure activities.
7. Stick to your schedule and reward yourself for achieving your study goals.

   ☆ WARNING: *Do not allow yourself to study too much.* Schedule time for the other things that you want to do and stick to your schedule.

   ☆ *Learn how to make yourself stop studying!* When you reach the scheduled time to stop, go get some exercise or do whatever you want to do. *Practice being a self-stopper!*

Yes, you read us right. For many students, the problem is not studying too little, they study so much they are inefficient.

C. Northcoat Parkinson observed that "work expands to fill available time." You may have experienced this phenomenon with a project such as cleaning up the house. Let's say that you had in mind cleaning up the house during three hours available on Saturday morning. If you have three hours available for cleaning up the house, it will probably take you three hours to get the job done.

But let's say that before you start to work Saturday morning, you learn that a very special person is coming by to visit and will arrive in about 30 minutes. You would probably be able to clean the house reasonably well in fewer than 30 minutes. What we suggest is that you decide what has to be done, do it, and then stop.

Time management experts often say that things not worth doing are not worth doing well. With less important jobs or matters don't waste precious time doing them as well as you can. Do them fast and quickly, just good enough to get by. Use your precious time for more important things.

A weekly study schedule such as the one we have at the end of the book will show you that you have many more hours during the day than you might have ever realized. If you don't have access to a commercially prepared weekly calendar with the time broken down by the hour, you can cut ours out and copy it.

Make Daily "To Do" Lists

Take a few minutes each evening to list the important things that you have to do the next day. List those things most important to be done. Then plan ahead. Here's what one student reports doing:

> On a daily scale, I prepare myself by getting my book bag ready to go out the door the night before. I make sure I have paper, pens, books, calculator—everything I will need for the next day's classes. This saves much searching time and also reduces stress the next morning. Along with all the supplies I *will* need, I make sure there is nothing in my bag that I *won't* need. This includes extra books, note pads, tennis shoes, a broken door handle—anything just along for the ride.

Your "to do" list gives you a good frame of reference during the day. It reminds you what to do and what to say "no" to. It also lets you know when you are done.

Get in the habit of putting your time and energy into your highest priority items. Don't kid yourself that you will get to the really big project after you clean up and or with all the little things. By the time you finish the little, unimportant tasks your time is gone and you are too tired to work on the important project. The same student quoted above says:

> To me the most important thing is *putting first things first*. A set study time is a priority. Once time is decided upon, decide what needs to be done and *do it*. One way I can remind myself of the importance of my commitments is to picture the result of my actions. I ask myself "How will watching TV instead of studying affect my future?" This puts things in perspective and reminds me of my priorities.

The Big Picture

Every person who is both busy and effective makes decisions about what to do and what not to do with their time...

You started with your dream.
You decided that going to college was the way to reach your dream of a better life.
You confront your fears and concerns.
You select courses that lead to what you want out of college.
You imagine yourself succeeding in your courses.
You identify what you have to do to pass each course.
You develop monthly and weekly schedules for doing what it takes to complete course requirements.
You make "to do" lists that help you focus on your highest priority activities each day.
You stick with your daily schedule.
You balance being a self-starter with being a self-stopper.
You succeed in college while still having time for your family, your job, and other important activities.

Action Review: Checklist for Time Management

☐ Do I have a calendar for the term marked with dates of all tests and assignments?

☐ Do I make weekly schedules of my classes and activities?

☐ Do I use daily "to do" lists?

☐ Can I do less important things quickly? Just good enough to get by?

☐ Do I set specific study goals for each course?

☐ Do I set up a schedule to achieve study goals?

☐ Do I stop studying when I said I would?

Success Group Activity

Show each other your schedules. Talk about your ways of managing your time well. Discuss how it feels to do so many things by the clock. Discuss what it feels like to be both a self-starter and a self-stopper.

Chapter 9

The Best Way to Study

Do you appreciate the value of asking good questions?

Do you know the most widely used and effective way to study?

Do you know that your studying time can be reduced by reading to answer questions?

Have you arranged a good study area for yourself?

Do you use principles of psychology on yourself when you study?

What Psychologists Know About Learning

Psychologists have studied how people learn for almost 100 years. You can use their research findings to improve your ability to learn and remember. Their research also helps show what interferes with learning and remembering.

Here are some important principles to understand:

- The weakest form of learning is *passive recognition*. Studying is not the same as reading your Sunday newspaper. Reading your textbook is not the same as reading a novel.
- The strongest form of learning is *active recall*. This learning method is to read the material with curiosity, intending to remember what you read, and then from memory write or verbally give a summary of what you learned. Passively reading your textbooks and lecture notes over and over again is no fun and is an inefficient way to learn.
- How well you first learn and then later recall what you study is influenced by your study environment and study plan.

The purpose of any test is to measure what you have learned. This means that to pass tests you must start by learning the information you will be tested on!

Textbooks are not written to entertain you. When it comes to studying, you must use study techniques that motivate you to mentally reach out and grasp important information.

Asking and Answering Questions: The Key to Efficient Learning and Success in Classes

Let's look at a simple and highly effective learning technique. Thousands of students using this technique find that once they learn to ask and answer questions when they study they become highly successful in school. They save hundreds of hours studying, have more time to spend with their families, hold jobs, take trips, attend concerts, and lead a balanced life.

Learning this study technique will take some effort. You may have to change many of your old habits. Such changes are sometimes difficult. In the long run, however, the benefit is worth the effort so stick with it.

Increase Your Reading Speed and Comprehension in Textbooks Using the SQ3R Method

The fastest way to spend less time reading assignments is to learn how to figure out the important questions and answers as quickly as possible. The following steps will increase your learning speed, comprehension and memory. Here is how to do it:

Skim—Question—Read—Recite—Review = SQ3R

Experts on study skills have found that the SQ3R method is the most efficient and effective means for getting the most out of reading material in the least amount of time.

Skim and Question

The purpose of skimming through a chapter is to determine what important questions are answered in the textbook chapter.

First, look at the beginning of the chapter to see whether or not there are chapter objectives or a list of questions. Read them.

Second, look at the end of the chapter to see if there is a chapter summary. If so, read it right away! This is where you will find the important points that authors wish to stress.

☆ When reading textbooks you decrease your study time by reading the summary at the end of the chapter before reading the chapter!

Third, skim through the chapter quickly. How do you skim a chapter? Glance through the chapter rapidly. You want a picture of the forest before you examine any trees. Look for titles, subtitles, illustrations, pictures, charts, highlighted words or phrases, and questions that will give you a basic idea of what the chapter is about.

Fourth, turn titles, subtitles, and highlighted terms into questions while you skim. For instance, "Maslow's Hierarchy of Needs" is a section heading in a psychology textbook. You simply ask "What is the hierarchy of needs that Maslow described?"

By asking questions as you skim, you keep yourself alert to the important points in the chapter. Reading in this manner is active rather than passive. As you skim, try to ask questions that, when answered, will give you a good summary of the chapter.

What does a good question look like? It usually starts with a phrase like:

Name three kinds of...
_____ is an example of...
Describe the ways that...
List the important points about...
The pioneering research was done by...
The research proved...
What does _____ mean?
The definition of _____ is...

Read to Answer Questions

It is now time to read: Read as quickly as you can. Read to find the answers to questions you have generated while surveying the chapter.

☆ In many instances, your questions and answers will be in titles, subtitles, or lead sentences and chapter summaries.

When reading to answer questions, read selectively. Read to find answers to questions. As you read, when you come to the answer to a question that you hadn't predicted, slow down, ask the new question, and make sure you know the answer. When you come to material you already know, skip over it.

Recite Answers and Summaries

After you read the chapter to answer your questions, close the book. Write a short summary of what you have just read. You learn best when you both write your summary and recite it out loud from memory. The more sensory systems and muscles you involve in your learning the faster and more long lasting your learning will be.

Many students start a new chapter before proving to themselves that they learned the contents of the chapter they just read. They think, "I read it, I underlined it, I know what it's about." *Don't make that mistake!* Prove to yourself that you comprehend the chapter by answering questions out loud and writing chapter summaries.

☆ Underlining or using a yellow highlighter will not lead to remembering nearly as well as writing or reciting what you know!

Make a List of Terms and Concepts

The fastest way to master a new subject is to learn what the terms and concepts mean. To accomplish this quickly, make a list of words, terms, principles, and concepts that you will be expected to define, explain, describe, or understand.

Many students find that 3 x 5 cards are useful. You write the term, concept, or principle on one side of the card. On the reverse side you write out the definition or explanation. Then, when it is time to recite and review what you know, you look at the card and try to state or write from memory the definition written out on the other side.

Using 3 x 5 cards is handy because you can carry them around with you instead of your textbook. When you have a few minutes after lunch, on the bus, or while waiting for a class to start you can use the time to review your knowledge of definitions.

☆ You do not need long blocks of time to study. You can study for a few minutes any time, any place!

Review

If you have followed the steps so far, you are in excellent shape to review what you've learned at any time. And, as you will see in the next chapter, you are also prepared to write practice questions. The SQ3R method is simple, it saves time, and it works!

The Benefits

A major benefit from using SQ3R is that you study for a limited time and then stop with a feeling of confidence that you know the material! You spend less time rereading chapters and doing other time-consuming study activities. This study method gives you the feeling that you've mastered the material. When you know you can answer questions correctly and make accurate summaries, you feel confident.

Some Difficulties of SQ3R

It can be difficult to change old reading habits. You may be used to reading every word, afraid that you're going to miss something. A new technique such as the SQ3R method may appear reckless because you learn so fast. It takes more energy to ask questions and write summaries than it does to passively read printed pages. You have to space your studying across many weeks.

Advantages of SQ3R

On the other hand, with SQ3R you spend less time memorizing. You don't waste time rereading and looking at material you already know. You focus on learning the key concepts. You don't waste time looking for unimportant details.

Your studying is organized and structured. You achieve your study goals and move on.

Athletes Practice

The SQ3R method is similar to the way that athletes prepare for competition. Imagine yourself agreeing to run in a 10 kilometer race several months from now. You will run with friends and it is important for all of you to do well. To be at your best, would you loaf around until the last few days and then prepare by running day and night until the time of the race? No. You'd start now with a weekly schedule of jogging and running. A little bit of practice on a regular basis prepares you the best. The same approach is true for effective studying and remembering.

Try the study techniques, and look for the following results:

- The quality of your questions and answers will improve with practice.

- The amount of time it takes you to ask questions and write good summaries will decrease.
- You will be able to cover large amounts of material in far less time.
- You will find that you think up the same questions that your instructors ask.
- Your study periods will be shorter and you will feel comfortable stopping when your study goals have been reached.

Your Study Area

The environment you study in affects how well you learn. Here are some tips about what to do and not do:

Study in the same place at home and at school. Don't keep changing your studying locations. New places distract you.

Create a study area for yourself at home. Do whatever you can to make it the place where your attention is devoted entirely to your studying. If you study at a desk, keep it cleared off.

Use a comfortable chair. It will be a good investment to get a comfortable chair that adjusts for height and back support. Discomfort can lead to muscle strain and physical distractions.

Arrange good lighting. To reduce eye strain, your room should be well lit, with the main light source off to one side. A light directly behind or in front of you will be reflected from the glossy pages of your textbooks. A constant glare tires your eyes more quickly than indirect lighting. If you can't shift the lamp, shift your desk. Place the desk so that no portion of the bulb shines directly into your eyes.

If you wear glasses, consider having them tinted slightly. Older eyes are vulnerable to eye strain.

> I loved my study area. My kids kept giving me posters to hang on the wall, and soon I felt that my corner was like the typical student's study area. Over my desk was my favorite Tom Sellek *Magnum PI* poster with Tom standing on the beach wearing shorts. Tom and I spent a lot of hours together, and I can still visualize that poster.—MK

Mask Auditory Distractions

Use steady background sounds to mask distracting noises. Play your radio or stereo softly while you study to create a steady background of "noise" to mask occasional sounds. Experiment with stations or records until you find what works best for you. FM radio stations playing instrumental music are usually best.

☆ Don't try to study with the television on.

If you want to watch a TV program, then watch it. But don't try to avoid feeling guilty about watching television by having your book open to read during commercials. Studying with the TV set on is academic suicide. Use television time as a reward after you have completed a study period, if you wish.

Work With Your Concentration Span

Have you ever sat reading for awhile and then suddenly realized you didn't know what you just read? That your mind wasn't paying attention to what your eyes were reading? This is not an uncommon experience for students.

The problem is that while you can make yourself sit and read hour after hour, your mind will take a break when it needs one. You are a human being. The length of time you can make your mind concentrate on a subject is limited. Even if you can make your body sit at a desk for hours, your mind will take breaks.

The way to make your study time more productive is to start with what you can do now and build on that. On the average, how long can you study before your mind slips off to something else? Twenty-five minutes? Ten minutes? Most students can concentrate on a textbook 10 to 15 minutes before starting to daydream.

Record Your Study Time Segments

The next time you study, use a note pad on your desk. Write down the time when you start. Then record approximately how long you can read your textbook before your mind starts to daydream. Don't set any particular goals for yourself yet. First, we have to find out what is the typical amount of time you spend reading textbook materials before your mind starts to wander.

Let's say that you find your average concentration span is about 12 minutes. Accept that as your current level. Don't be bothered or upset thinking that you can't control your mind. Focus instead on increasing your concentration span in small, reasonable amounts.

Take Mandatory Breaks

Once you determine your concentration span, set up a study schedule that fits your current ability. Take a brief break after each study segment and a long break about once an hour.

You will probably find the end of a study segment coming so quickly you will be tempted to continue. *Don't continue without your break!* Keep your agreement with yourself. When you decide to take a short break after each 15 minute segment, then do so. *Do not allow yourself to study more than the allotted time.*

When you promise your mind a break after 15 minutes, keep your word! No matter how much you want to keep on, make yourself take a short break. Get up and stretch. Get a drink of water or step outside for a breath of fresh air before starting the next study segment.

Mix Study Subjects

Here are more principles of learning:

- When you learn one set of facts and then follow it with similar facts or material, the second set will interfere with your memory of the first and the first will interfere with your memory of the second.
- When you try to learn lots of information at one time you remember the first items and the last items best. The middle is most difficult to recall.

When Steve came into the learning center he was tired and discouraged. He worked full time, was enrolled in three night courses, and studied many hours evenings and weekends. As hard as he studied, however, he found it difficult to remember the material the way he felt he should.

Did Steve have a memory problem? No. His problem was that he would study one subject all evening or all morning and then switch to another subject the next day.

The more you try to learn similar material at one time, the worse your recall will be. How can you avoid this problem when you have lots of material to study? The best way is to mix your study hours with dissimilar material.

☆ Do not devote one long study period to one subject.

Switch subjects about once an hour. Always try to make your new subject as different as possible from the subject you have just finished. That way your mind can be assimilating one topic while you are reading about another.

Principles of Learning in Action

Here is an example of a study schedule using the principles described above:

15 min.—history
2 min. stretch break
15 min.—history
2 min. stretch break
15 min.—history
10 min. break—go to bathroom, drink some water, walk around
15 min.—math
2 min. stretch break
15 min.—math
2 min. stretch break
15 min.—math
10 min. break—get fruit juice and carrots, short phone call
15 min.—English Lit.
2 min. stretch break
15 min.—English Lit.
2 min. stretch break

15 min. English Lit.

All done! Reward—watch video tape of Bill Cosby show.

Now that you know how to use the principles of learning to study efficiently and effectively, the next chapter will cover how to prepare for tests.

Action Review: Checklist for Successful Studying

Here is a list of guidelines that will help you to monitor your studying and your success at implementing the learning strategies we've described.

☐ Do I use the SQ3R method for learning course material?

☐ Do I skim chapters first, ask questions, read the summaries, and then read to answer questions?

☐ Do I practice writing answers to questions and write chapter summaries?

☐ Do I make up lists of terms and concepts to use when I test my ability to recite definitions from memory?

☐ Have I created a good study area for myself?

☐ Do I study in short time periods and take breaks?

☐ Do I switch study subjects often?

☐ Do I reward myself when I have successfully accomplished my study goals?

Success Group Activity

Talk with each other about your study methods. After using the SQ3R method talk about your results. Find out what your study areas at home are like. Talk about how you handle distractions. Compliment each other for efforts and progress.

Chapter 10

How to Get
High Grades on Tests

Do you know that successful students make and take practice tests?

Do you know that you can reduce nervousness if you feel free to write comments on tests about test items?

Do you know that you can ask instructors about test items during the examination?

How to Guarantee Your Success on Tests

Have you ever taken an exam that didn't require you to answer questions? Of course not. Your grades are determined by your ability to answer questions, not by your pleasant personality!

To do well in college, you have to be able to answer questions asked by your instructors. That's why we emphasize that every time you read your course notes or texts, you should look for potential exam questions.

If you want to do well on your exams, spend your study time developing exam questions from notes and texts. Then test yourself to see whether you can pass the test items you created.

Few students prepare for exams by taking practice tests. Most students prepare for exams by reading, underlining, and rereading their lecture notes and texts. But no instructor conducts an exam by asking you to read your notes or textbook to him or her. Your instructors ask you to answer questions based on their lecture notes, readings, and the textbook. The point is obvious:

☆ If you want to do well on tests, always study as though you're practicing to take a test.

Make and Take Practice Tests

Pretend you are teaching the course. Make up exams just like the exams you believe your instructors will give. Just as orchestras rehearse for concerts and football teams play practice games, prepare for exams by taking exams.

Practicing the same kind of test items you will be required to answer in a test situation helps you relax. It builds your confidence. You feel less tension about tests. You know you have studied the right questions, and you sleep better knowing you've studied correctly.

How to Predict Exam Questions

What kinds of questions should you ask? Questions just like the questions your instructor will ask on exams. Successful students, as noted earlier, begin a course by asking *when* tests will be given and *what kind* they will be.

Will the test be multiple-choice? True-false? Short or long essay? A combination of these? Write your practice tests using the same kinds of questions.

You have read in previous chapters that the best way to study textbooks and lecture notes is to view them as answers to questions. There are other sources of exam questions as well. They include: old exams, instructors, classmates, discussion groups, and student manuals.

Old Exams

Don't feel guilty about looking over past exams. Looking at old exams tells you what an instructor thinks is important information for which students should be responsible.

Looking at old exams doesn't guarantee that you'll know exactly what your exam questions will be. Exams change from semester to semester because instructors change their lectures, textbooks, films, approaches, and even their viewpoints. Nevertheless, by looking at old exams you may find out:

1. Does the instructor have some favorite questions that he or she asks every year?
2. Do test questions appear to be taken from material similar to what I am studying?
3. Do test questions come primarily from lecture notes or from a variety of sources?
4. What types of questions does the instructor prefer: multiple-choice, short-answer, true-false, essay?

Student Manuals

Student manuals that accompany many textbooks are excellent sources of exam questions. Student manuals contain true-false, multiple-choice, fill-in, and short essay questions. Even if your exam will be made up of questions that differ in style, the manual questions are still valuable.

Note: *The publisher of your textbook may have a student manual available even if the instructor did not require its use.* Check this out—especially for introductory textbooks. If a student manual exists, you can purchase it through the bookstore or directly from the publisher.

Discussion Groups

Some of the best sources of test questions can be fellow students. By talking with other students enrolled in the course or with students who have been enrolled in past semesters, you can get an excellent perspective on the types of questions and answers you should be looking for.

Instructors

Your instructor can be a good source of information about test questions. Many students find it difficult to ask instructors what they believe is important. As we said earlier, most instructors are happy to tell you what questions they think are important. Give them a chance. Ask them!

Create a File of Practice Tests

Write out your practice questions on sheets of paper separate from your lecture notes. If you use 3x5 cards, place your questions on one side and your answers on the other.

This system will allow you to quiz yourself quickly. You look at your questions, provide written or oral answers, and then check to see how well your quiz answers compare to your original answers.

Most students like this system because it gives them a central filing system of questions and answers. Rather than fumbling through lecture notes and textbooks, they go to their notebooks of questions and answers or their stacks of question cards and quiz themselves.

How to Quiz Yourself

Here is how to make and take practice tests:

1. Determine the length of the exam. Will it be a short, 20-item, true-false quiz? A 60-item multiple-choice test? A one-hour essay test?
2. Arrange the questions you've been accumulating from chapters, lecture notes, study groups, old exams, and other sources into practice tests.
3. Take your practice tests under conditions as similar as possible to those under which you'll be tested. The classroom in which you'll be tested is a good place.
4. Answer your questions without referring to your books or other sources of information.
5. If you are not sure of the answer to an item, try to guess. Make up answers as if you were in a real testing situation, trying to earn at least partial credit.
6. After you complete your practice test, compare your answers with those that you have in your own set of questions and answers.
7. After noting the questions you have answered well and those in need of improvement, revise your test.

Another way to take practice tests is to have a friend or family member quiz you. Later, when you feel ready, get together with several classmates and quiz each other.

Weekly and Final Practice Tests

If you take weekly practice tests in each subject area, you'll find that exam panic and last minute cramming are a thing of the past. Taking weekly tests allows you to master small amounts of information each week and then to put everything together in a final practice test just before you take the real thing.

Before each scheduled test, take a comprehensive practice test made up of sample questions from your weekly tests. You'll be pleasantly surprised at how much easier it is to pass your final practice test when you have been taking weekly tests.

The Advantages of Practice Tests

SQ3R may appear to be time consuming, but it isn't. Predicting exam questions is the most useful technique you can use for learning the important concepts covered in your courses. Students who collect test questions and answers, take weekly practice tests and take final practice tests spend far less time on irrelevant and wasteful studying. These students practice exactly what their instructors will require of them, asking and answering questions.

Such students also obtain a more solid education. They remember what they have learned much better than students who cram for exams. The research into forgetting shows that people quickly forget most of what they learn unless they review and rehearse the material.

These study methods help you pass tests well and obtain an excellent education. Your success in life, after all, is a matter of what you know and what you can do, not of your grades. When you go to an attorney to have a contract drawn up, do you ask "What grade did you receive in contract law?" If you have a pulled muscle, do you ask the physical therapist about his or her scores on anatomy tests? No. You seek help or services on the basis of what people know and can do.

> Some instructors will use test questions you write—especially well-written multiple choice or true-false items. It never hurts to ask the instructor if he or she would like to see questions you've written. Be sure to include chapter and page references, and mark the correct alternative. What a boost to sit down to a test and see *your* questions on it!—MK

Taking Your Instructors' Tests

Now that you know how to prepare for a test, let's make sure that you know how to relax and use your time wisely once you have the real test in your hands.

General Guidelines

1. Read the instructions to determine the types of questions you'll be expected to answer. Determine where you'll earn the most points. Form a basic idea of how the test is set up, and decide what you will do.
2. Plan your time to ensure that you will get to all parts of the test. Do not devote too much time to the difficult parts and then panic when you find that you can't complete the whole test.
3. Before starting, determine whether or not answering the easier questions will earn you just as many points as answering the more difficult questions. If so, complete the easy questions first. After answering them you'll have more confidence, and you will be able to pass on to the more difficult questions.
4. Make sure you understand what each question is asking. If the directions say, "Give several examples of...," then do exactly that! Give instructors exactly what they ask for.
5. If you don't understand a question or find it extremely difficult, place an X by it, and move on to easier questions. You can come back later. This procedure saves time and prevents anxiety. Most important, you may find the answer hidden in other questions as you move through the test. Expect the answer to come to you as you work on other items, just as you do when trying to recall a person's name. Relaxing and expecting the answer to come to you in a few moments works better than struggling to remember.

Answering Objective Questions

Tests using multiple-choice, true-false, and matching items are called *objective* tests. They are objective because they prevent subjective feelings in the test grader from increasing or decreasing your score.

Read objective questions carefully, but answer them quickly. If the answer is not immediately obvious to you, put a mark by the item and come back to it later. Other items in a test often give clues to the answers in earlier items.

Never leave an answer blank, unless there is a penalty for guessing.

Contrary to the popular advice about never changing answers, it can be to your advantage to *change answers* . The research shows that when students have prepared well for an examination the number of students who gain by changing answers is significantly greater than the number of students who lose by changing answers. Be careful about changing answers, of course. But your second thought, if you have prepared well, has a good chance of being correct.

Multiple-Choice Questions. When you answer a multiple-choice question, eliminate the obviously incorrect answers first. You will save considerable time and increase your chance of choosing the correct answer.

Read and answer each question quickly. Pay attention to key words and phrases such as "Which is *not...*" or "*According to* Skinner..." or "The *strongest* evidence..." After you have answered all questions, go back to see if you read them correctly. Finish by going back to those that you marked with X the first time through because you were unsure of the answers.

Matching Questions. Check to make sure you have read the directions for matching questions carefully. Sometimes students believe that matches are so obvious that they do exactly the opposite of what is asked. If the instructions say, "Match those that are different" or "Match those that are opposite," you'll feel rather foolish if you have spent a lot of time matching those that are similar.

Answer the easy ones first. This tactic reduces the chance of guessing incorrectly on more difficult matches.

True-False Questions. Never waste a lot of time pondering true-false questions. Many students have been known to waste major portions of test periods attempting to solve true-false questions as if they were Chinese puzzles. If an answer isn't immediately apparent, don't become frustrated. Simply move on to the next question. One or two questions aren't worth that many points.

Written Examinations

Written examinations tend to be of two types, long essays and short answer tests. Long essay examinations ask you to "Trace the development of..." At most schools an essay examination will require you to write from five to ten essays. (Note: If the instructor indicates that it is a blue book examination, this means you must purchase from the bookstore and bring to class a book with a blue cover designed specifically for writing examination essays.)

Long Essay Questions. Outline your answer to an essay question before writing it. In this way you will ensure that you include key ideas for which you will earn points from the grader. A well-written essay answer usually includes the following:

1. **Introduction**. Begin with several paragraphs that ask the most important questions or present the main issues. It can help to pretend that you are writing a short article and need an interesting opening.
2. **Define terms**. Define what you mean when you use certain terms. Be sure to call attention to conflicting viewpoints or any uncertainties in your mind about the question asked. This approach often clarifies for the instructor why you have answered the question in a particular manner.
3. **Use subheadings** As you write, be sure to use subheadings for longer answers. Subheadings show you and the reader the organization in your answer.
4. **Give examples.** Use examples to support your main points. You demonstrate that you really know what you are taking about if you can present examples to substantiate your position.
5. **Conclusions** Summarize and draw conclusions. But note, *do not* include any new data, points, or examples in the conclusion! Add new questions, perhaps, but no new information.
6. **Edit for clarity.** After you have finished writing, pretend that you are the grader. Ask yourself, "Have I misread or misunderstood the questions? Did I leave anything out?

Have I made any careless mistakes?" Allot time at the end to polish answers, refine points, and deal with more difficult questions that have puzzled you.

Short-Answer Tests. Short-answer tests may contain from 20 to 40 items usually worth from one to eight points each. Such tests may ask you to

- Define each of the terms and concepts in a list
- Outline an experiment or study
- List the main points in favor of a procedure
- Give three criticisms against...
- Draw and correctly label a chart or structure (such as a nerve cell)
- Summarize the views of an author or scientist
- Name the basic steps or stages in a process

Most of your answers on short-answer tests will be incomplete sentences and phrases. Long paragraphs are not what the instructor asked for. Most instructors appreciate clear, legible, easily read lists of phrases. If you want to jot down some of the lists and other information you have memorized use the back of the exam.

When Questions Puzzle You

What can you do when you come to a question that baffles you? Remember that in your reading you've probably read some information that is relevant. Put down *anything* and you'll probably earn a few points, which is more than you'll have if you leave the answer blank. While taking the exam, you're likely to recall or see some information related to the answer you need. If you can't figure out the exact answer, you can probably come close.

You Can Write Comments About the Test

If, in spite of all your excellent preparation, you are still a bit nervous about the test, try imagining that the following statement is written across the top of the test: "Feel free to write comments about the test items."

Wilbert J. McKeachie, a psychologist known for his research on ways to improve teaching, discovered that when that statement was printed at the top of tests, many students did better. An interesting result was that it didn't matter whether students actually wrote anything about the test or not! The presence of the statement alone was enough to improve the scores of students who had fears of failing.[1]

You Can Ask Questions During the Exam

Instructors know that questions are not always clear. Sometimes a question isn't worded well. That's why most instructors will answer questions about test questions during exams.

If there are one or two questions that just don't make sense, go ask the instructor. Ask "I don't remember this material being covered. Could you give me some help?" "Where was this information presented in the textbook?" "The way this item is worded, there are several possible answers, this one and this one. Which do you want?"

If you are drawing a blank anyway, you have nothing to lose by seeing if the instructor will give you some hints. He or she will not give you the answer, but a comment like "That item is from the chart at the end of Chapter 6" may give you the clue you need.

The Advantages of These Test-Taking Methods

The methods described in this chapter can improve your confidence taking tests. Students who use these techniques get good grades on tests because they:

1. Seldom misread the test questions or answer questions incorrectly.
2. Do not waste time on questions that stump them.
3. Do not answer questions with irrelevant information.
4. Often get points on questions that require them to "bull" a little.
5. Seldom develop exam panic.
6. Rarely fail tests (they usually receive B or better).

7. Receive more points for answers than predicted.
8. Feel more relaxed and confident while taking tests.
9. Seldom leave out important information from answers.
10. Are able to complete exams in the allotted time.
11. Get higher grades in their courses.

One Final Tip

It is not necessary to play the suffering student game. Learning can be pleasant. Studying for exams can be efficient if you use the principles we've just discussed. If you prepare well for exams, then the night before each exam you can relax and do one more very helpful thing: *get a good night's sleep!*

Action Review: Checklist for Success in Preparing for and Taking Tests

☐ Do I practice quizzing myself on possible test questions?

☐ Do I make up and take practice tests?

☐ Do I practice taking tests under conditions as similar as possible to those under which I will be tested?

☐ When I take tests, do I use the techniques suggested in this chapter?

Success Group Activity

Talk about taking tests. How do you feel on the way to the test? What do you say to yourself when you walk into the room and sit waiting for the tests to be passed out? What is your way of handling taking tests?

If you've all taken several tests, show each other your test results. Talk about how well you handled yourself and what you could do better next time.

Chapter 11

How to Write Excellent Papers

Do you know your starting point when writing papers should be, "What questions am I trying to answer in this paper?"

Do you know that the ability to write excellent papers depends on how well you know how to use the library?

Do you know which librarian to talk to when you need help?

Do you know that the difference between a barely acceptable paper and one that is excellent is determined by your ability to revise and rewrite?

Writing Papers for Instructors

The successful way to write papers closely parallels the steps you take in preparing for tests. Begin by listing questions that might serve as a basis for an interesting paper.

When you approach writing from this perspective, the process is less difficult and less time consuming. More important, your papers are focused, accurate, and well liked by instructors. Here are the steps to follow:

Pick Your Topic and Check with Your Instructor

Try to pick the topic that is both interesting for you and one that your instructor believes is important. If you listen closely in class, you will often detect an instructor's real interests. In selecting a topic, take your instructor's interests into account. Then go talk to your instructor. Ask for advice on how to proceed. Is your topic workable? Is it important? Are there problems to watch out for? Which issues are too simple and which are too complicated for you to tackle? Ask for a bibliography. Ask for suggestions on how to get started. If you ask good questions, your instructor's answers may provide you with a ready-made outline of your project.

Remember Your Audience

Always keep in mind that you are writing to an audience of one, your instructor. You are not writing an article for *Reader's Digest* nor for your school paper. You are writing to your instructor, and you need to demonstrate to *this* person what you understand about the assignment.

You have a better chance of doing well if you take time to find out exactly what you need to do to get a good evaluation. If your instructor is vague or unwilling to talk with you about what you plan for your paper, talk to students who have taken the course in the past. Try to read papers that other students have written for this instructor. That will give you an idea about how your instructor evaluates student work.

Ask Your Questions

Ask yourself, "What important questions should I answer in the paper if I wish to cover the topic adequately?" Narrow your topic so that your research has a specific focus.

Begin your paper by indicating the specific questions you intend to deal with. Explain why these questions are important.

If you aren't certain how to start, go to the library. Find a reference librarian. They are wonderful people to know. They can help you find sources of information you probably wouldn't think of. They know the library thoroughly. Most want to help you. That is what they are paid for. Make use of their expertise.

An excellent way to start a research project is to first consult *Encyclopedia Britannica*. If it covers the subject, this encyclopedia will often give a good introductory summary of it and the standard views concerning it. This encyclopedia can help focus a research project very quickly.

Skim through the most recent books and journals that deal with your topic. Even new books can be several years behind the most current research, so it is wise to go to journals that are more up to date. By looking at what the experts are doing, you are likely to get a better idea of the important questions currently being investigated.

Once you have a list of good questions, start looking for answers. The best place to search is the library.

How to Use Your Library Well

Libraries are wonderful places. They are one of the human race's most important memory banks. You can discover extraordinary ideas, even whole new worlds and facts about every conceivable subject. Do you know how to access this information? Do you know how libraries work?

Microfiche and Computer, On-Line Search Systems

In most college libraries your search for references will start with the Microfiche system or a computer terminal. Microfiche is a piece of photographic film, usually 4 X 6 inches, that has to be magnified for reading.

The more modern libraries now have an on-line computer system that records the daily availability of books and journals. If you are unsure how to use the microfiche or the terminals, ask a librarian for help.

Beginning Your Library Search

Libraries index their books in three ways: by author, subject, and title. Which should you start with?

Let's say your paper is going to be about nutrition and athletic performance. You've heard about high protein diets and carbohydrate loading and seen ads for vitamin supplements. You've heard about professional athletes on vegetarian diets and seen athletes eating Wheaties. How do you find out what the facts are?

With your questions in mind, you'll probably want to start with the subject index.

Use your imagination when looking through the subject index. Look under every topic you can think of—nutrition, dieting, physical education, health science, and so on. Make notes of book titles and authors, and always write down the complete call number of the book. The *call number* is the library's code number that tells you exactly where the book is shelved.

If a book has the statement "reference" or "reference desk," you will not find the book in the open shelves. An instructor has probably placed the book on reserve so that it can be checked out only for several hours.

Another possibility is to ask the reference librarian to run a computer search on your topic. Computer searches can cost. If your subject is focused enough, the cost can be less than $20, even less than $10. A computer search is very efficient and can save you hours of preliminary work.

Periodical Index

The most up-to-date information, especially scientific reports on research, appears in professional journals long before it is reported in books. Look for titles of journals that would contain articles related to your topic. For your paper you'd cover all the nutrition and physical education journals.

The journals of national professional groups are often titled *The American...* or *National Society of...* or *The Journal of the American...* So be sure to look under "American," "National," and "Journal" in the alphabetical listings.

As you record call numbers for books and journals, you will begin to see a pattern. The books and journals with relevant information will be clustered in two or three places in the library. When you go to these sections, you will discover other books and journals that you didn't see in the catalog indexes.

Read first to get a general orientation. When you find useful data or passages you may want to quote in your paper, record your source and quote accurately. It can be very frustrating later when you can't remember which author you quoted or which statement is your own summary. Most libraries have coin-operated photocopying equipment available. Save time by using it.

From the journal articles you will learn about books to look for. From the books you will learn about the journals that focus on your topic most frequently. In a book you may learn about an older journal article that is exactly what you need. You may discover, for example, that an article on blood sugar and endurance was published in a medical journal.

Reference Section

You still haven't used your library well, however, if you ignore another source of useful information. It is the reference section. In the reference section you will find many resources, in addition to encyclopedias. Of most interest right now, however, is the *Reader's Guide to Periodical Literature*.

This index lists in alphabetical order the titles of articles published in the major popular magazines. If an article on nutrition and athletic performance has appeared in *Business Week*, *American Health*, or *Runner's World*, the *Reader's Guide* will list it. Some scientific researchers publish directly in popular publications so don't discount magazines as a source of information.

Besides, the information is usually easier to understand than in professional journals and books. If you don't find the information you need or want in your library, try other libraries.

Look for Answers

You'll soon discover that by having questions in mind that you want to answer, you can quickly cut through the massive amount of material that could otherwise distract you. By reading to answer your questions, you save precious hours that might otherwise be lost in meandering around, wondering how much you should include in your paper.

Expect New Questions

In the process of answering questions, new questions may arise. You may find that as you do your research you need to change the original questions in some way or add some new ones.

Write Your Paper

Now that you've gathered your information, it is time to write the answers to your questions.

Write the answers to your questions as precisely as possible. Be brief. Don't include irrelevant information. Make your point and back it with sufficient examples and data. Draw inferences and discuss the implications of the information. Answers to questions are more believable when they are precise and well documented. Let your reader know that you've done research on the answers.

Quote experts in the field. The more authoritative your examples, the better you will be able to convince your reader.

Brief, accurate quotations are more effective in supporting your points than lengthy quotations. Brief quotations, figures, and specific facts are more persuasive than vague generalizations.

Give precise references for your information sources. From your references, the reader should be able to find the specific page of your source.

Arrange Your Answers

Once you have written your answers, arrange them so that they build upon one another. Your next task is to connect them by saying, showing, explaining, or demonstrating how they are related to each other. These transitions from answer to answer should be brief but complete.

When you have arranged your answers and connected them, briefly summarize what you have written. The summary will tell you what you have done in your paper and will provide you with your paper's overall focus or central idea. Now check your summary against how you began your paper. Do they match?

The Steps So Far

1. Determine which questions you will answer in your paper.
2. Describe the intent of your paper and the questions that you will answer.
3. Answer each question as precisely and authoritatively as possible. Provide examples to support your position.
4. Document your sources in footnotes and a bibliography.
5. Put your answers in sequence so that they build upon one another.
6. Provide transitions from answer to answer.
7. Summarize what you have written and check the summary against what you described as the intent of the paper.

Rewrite Your Paper

After you write your first draft, make an appointment to go over it with your instructor. Many instructors will give you good feedback about whether you are ready to type the final draft or need further revision.

The real writing of any paper takes place when you revise. Most writers produce several rough drafts before attempting their final version.

☆ Plan from the beginning to produce a rough draft which you will then revise into your final copy.

This way you can produce your first draft quickly and won't be wasting time going back trying to edit, correct typing mistakes, and such as you write out or type your first draft.

When you are ready to rewrite your paper, you should

1. Make sure you have clearly indicated the questions your paper will answer.
2. Ask yourself if the questions you have selected are important to the topic and cover it well.
3. Ask yourself how effectively you have answered the questions.
4. Ask yourself if you recognize what makes your writing interesting, not so interesting, confusing, or on track.
5. Correct any grammatical, punctuation, or spelling errors.
6. Refine any answers.
7. Decide how you want to conclude the paper. Consider including statements about what you learned in the process of writing the paper and why writing it was a valuable experience for you.
8. Have your instructor look over your rough draft.

If you feel that you need guidance, contact the English department. Most English departments run a writing skills center for non-English majors. It is worth looking into.

Caution: Never Plagiarize

Once in awhile, a student will copy passages from a book or article and turn in the paper as his or her own work. Trying to pass off someone else's work as your own is called plagiarism. It rarely succeeds. An article written by a student attempting to learn a subject is not like a paper written by an expert. Most instructors can tell when writing is not the student's own.

It's human nature to consider taking shortcuts, but plagiarizing is not worth the risk. Plagiarism is illegal and unethical. And the probability is high you'll get caught.

☆ The quickest way to flunk a course, get expelled from college, and earn a reputation that will haunt you for years is to plagiarize.

Make Your Papers Look Good

If you want a good grade, make your paper look good. Type all your papers. You can safely assume that the instructor prefers it. If you can't type, consider taking a typing class. In any case, typing is easy to learn and it is one of the best investments you can make in self-improvement.

English departments are headed in the direction of having their composition courses conducted as computer labs, so you might want to take an English composition course right away. It is a good way to develop computer literacy if you are not familiar with computers.

Present your writing in the most readable form. Instructors will accept papers printed out on computer printers. Make your typed copy as professional looking as possible. Use clean white paper, double space the lines, and make a minimum number of hand-written corrections on the typed copy.

Carefully follow any directions your instructor gives for footnotes, bibliographies, references, or other requirements. Your instructors usually have good reasons for them. There is nothing worse than devoting hours to a paper only to have it returned as incomplete. The consequences of failing to follow directions can be costly.

Make sure that your spelling and grammar are accurate. Use a dictionary when you are in doubt. Have someone else proofread your paper. Few things will bother instructors more than poor spelling and bad grammar. Studies have shown that instructors tend to give higher grades to papers that are expertly presented, clearly typed, grammatically correct, and free of spelling errors.[1]

A word to the wise: Turn in a paper that is the best that you can do. Be proud of your work! If your paper were a business report that would affect your chances of promotion, would you submit it the same way?

☆ NOTE : Always make a copy of your paper. The original could get damaged or lost. Play it safe. Keep a copy.

Action Review: Checklist for Success in Writing Papers and Using Your Library

☐ Do I write papers using the question and answer format?

☐ Have I asked the reference librarian for suggestions about where to look for information?

☐ Do I use the card catalog, microfiche, and on-line system to track down good reference sources?

☐ Do I get up-to-date information from professional journals?

☐ Do I use the *Reader's Guide*?

☐ Are my quotes and references accurate?

☐ When my first draft is completed, do I ask the instructor to look it over and give me suggestions for improvement?

☐ Do I check for correct grammar and spelling?

☐ Am I proud of what I hand in?

Success Group Activity

Talk about what you know about your college library. What tips do you have for each other about using the on-line system? If none of you know, then arrange for a demonstration by one of the librarians.

When you are developing ideas for papers, bounce topic ideas and key questions back and forth. Choose topics that are as interesting as possible.

After you have produced your first rough draft, show it to the others. Read each other's papers and ask questions. Point out strengths and parts done well. Give each other both suggestions and appreciation.

Chapter 12

Resolving Predictable Conflicts Between Instructors and Students

Do you know that you may be handicapping yourself with the attitude, "If only other people would change, my world would be a better place for me"?

Do you know that certain conflicts between students and instructors are predictable?

Do you know that difficulties in school frequently stem from a mismatch between an instructor's teaching style and students' learning style?

Do you know that your assumptions and attitudes about instructors can work for you or against you?

Predictable Conflicts Between Teaching and Learning Styles

Research into teaching effectiveness led psychologists to ask: "Why do some students do well with one instructor but not another?" and "Why do instructors do well with some students but not with others?"

Efforts to answer these questions uncovered a simple but relevant fact of academic life:

☆ The way some people teach doesn't always match up with the way other people learn.

Based on the research and on our own experiences, here are some differences between students and instructors that lead to some predictable conflicts, followed by suggestions on how to resolve the conflicts.

Auditory versus Visual Styles

Some people learn best by listening. Information doesn't stick well unless they hear it. Other people learn best by reading. They must see something before they believe it and remember it. What is your natural style?

Do you remember best what is said to you or what you read?
Do you prefer television or newspapers as your source of news?
Would you rather hear an expert talk on a subject or read what the expert has written?
If you have some spare time, would you rather sit around talking with people or go to the library and read?
If you are working with a group of people and there is some discrepancy between the written guidelines and the verbal instructions, which do you tend to believe?
Was reading the college catalog your main way of learning about your program and classes or did you merely skim the catalog and go see an advisor who told you everything you needed to know?

Based on your answers to these questions, which learning style do you prefer? Auditory or visual?

Everyone learns both ways, of course. It is not an either/or situation. Yet the differences between people are sometimes extreme enough to cause problems. If you have a visual learning style, you operate mainly on the basis of what you read. You may have difficulty with a verbal instructor who believes that telling people what to learn and know is sufficient.

Auditory Learning Style

If you have an auditory style, you will probably do well with an instructor who says everything to learn and do. You may have difficulty with a visually-oriented instructor who hands out a written statement about what to do to pass the course, who doesn't welcome discussion, and who assigns textbook material and outside readings that are never discussed in class.

The solution, if you have an auditory style in a class taught by a visually-oriented instructor is to:

1. Find classmates who will tell you what they learned from the textbook readings.
2. Dictate the main points from the reading assignments and handouts onto cassette tape and then listen to the tapes.
3. Consciously work at improving your ability to acquire information visually. For professional help, go to the reading improvement center.

Visual Learning Style

If you learn best visually, then you may be in trouble with an instructor who doesn't use handouts or doesn't write much on the blackboard. You may have problems with instructors who use class discussion as a teaching tool.

The solution if you have a visual orientation in a class taught by a verbal instructor is to:

1. Take good notes on what the instructor and your classmates say. After class fill in sentences and compare notes with other students.

2. Ask the instructor for suggested articles or books that will let you read the information you need to understand better.
3. Consciously work at listening and remembering what the instructor says. TIP: One woman wrote to us saying that she immediately typed out her lecture notes after every class.
4. If you are confused about a point, ask the instructor to tell you again and write down what you hear.

Right Brain versus Left Brain

Increased knowledge about the functions of the brain have changed the old views about how your brain operates. Years ago, students learned that the human brain (the cerebral cortex) has two halves. The newer view is to think of people as having two brains.

The left brain is where your speech center develops. Speech development is closely related to handedness. With some exceptions, if you are right handed your speech centers develop in your left brain. Once this occurs, many related functions develop in the left brain. Here is where you remember words, use logic, and think analytically about the world. The left brain makes possible your ability to think rationally and unemotionally. The left brain thinks in a linear fashion. It is time oriented.

The right brain carries your memory for music. You think visually, emotionally, and irrationally in the right brain. It is the source of creativity and intuition. Right-brain thinking follows emotional logic. Using it, you can visualize and think in patterns jumping from one spot in a pattern to another without apparent logic or reason.

If you tend to be a left-brain person, then you will be well matched to an instructor who gives you a thorough, unemotional listing of facts, data, analytic explorations, hypotheses, logic, evidence, numbers, definition of terms, and rational conclusions.

If you tend to be left brained and get an instructor who teaches in a right-brained way, you may find the course to be a bewildering experience. You may have experienced the instructor as weird, too emotional, and a bit nutty.

If you tend to be right brained with a left-brained teacher, the course will be painful for you. You'll feel like a thirsty person reaching for a glass of water only to discover that it is filled with sand.

☆ The solution to this sort of conflict, as we've stated before, is to avoid indulging in the attitude, "If only other people would change, my world would be a better place for me."

You can try to find someone (perhaps even the instructor) who can translate the material presented to you in a form that you can understand better. More important, however, we recommend that you work at gaining more use of your other brain.

The situation may not be easy at first, but it does give you a chance to add another dimension to yourself. And isn't this why you're in school?

You do not have to give up your more natural and preferred way of thinking, feeling, and talking. What you can do is add more to what you already have. We'll get into more of this in the chapter on the survivor personality.

Friendly versus Distant

Imagine your instructor stopping you as you leave the classroom and saying, "I liked the paper you turned in last week and want to talk with you about it. Do you have time to come and have a cup of coffee with me?"

How would you react? Would you be pleased and eagerly accept the invitation? Or would you draw back and make up an excuse to get away?

Just as it has been throughout your life, instructors and students vary considerably in regard to how friendly they want to be and how much distance they need to have. A friendly, extroverted instructor enjoys after-class contact with students. He or she will ask students to coffee, to evenings at the pizza house to talk and drink, and perhaps even to parties. If you are similarly friendly, then you are going to have a wonderful year.

If you are a more introverted person, however, you may

suffer from too much personal attention and closeness. You would much rather have a quiet, tactful instructor who respects your need to be left alone. Such an instructor understands how embarrassing it is to be called on to talk in class or to be openly praised for getting a high score on an exam.

On the other hand, if you are a basically friendly person with a more introverted instructor, you may find it puzzling to have him or her pulling away from you after class. After all, what are instructors for if not to be available for students? Yet your desire to be friendly may cause the instructor to stare at you and make an excuse to get away quickly. Then after that, you may be avoided.

The solution that we recommend was covered earlier in this chapter. If an instructor doesn't live up to your expectations about what an instructor should be like, then question your "shoulds." When reality is inconsistent with your beliefs and erroneous expectations, then what is the best solution?

Fallacies and Erroneous Beliefs About Instructors

Conflicts sometimes stem from assumptions students make about instructors. Here are some common assumptions students make. Check off the ones that apply to you:

☐ Most college instructors are trained in how to be effective instructors.

☐ Your instructors will always be well prepared for each class you attend.

☐ Every instructor will take a personal interest in you.

☐ Your instructors want all ideas challenged and want students to present their opinions and views during class.

☐ Instructors want you to obediently accept everything they say without reservation.

☐ Your instructors will know more than you and be able to answer all of your questions about a subject.

☐ Your instructors will give you a good grade if they like you.

The reality of going to college is that you'll attend courses taught by instructors with just about every human flaw imaginable. You'll attend courses taught by highly-competent instructors and less-capable instructors. That is simply the way things work.

☆ Your assumptions and attitudes about instructors will work for you or against you! You can complain about your instructors' deficiencies or you can attempt to get the most possible out of every course regardless of your instructors' personalities or lack of teaching competence. It is up to you!

External versus Internal Learning Styles

External learners are only open to believe information that comes from an authority or expert. Information or suggestions from other sources can't be trusted as accurate. If you prefer to get the guidance from expert sources and your instructor enjoys being an expert, then you have a good match.

The more you need an instructor who tells the class exactly what to learn, the better you will do with this type of instructor. If you need clear guidelines from instructors but take a course from someone who provides little direction, you may flounder. You may be sitting in class waiting for the instructor to tell you what the answer to a problem is, only to have him or her ask the class, "What do you think?" After the class talks for awhile, the instructor may refuse to say what the right answer is. He or she might say, "You may be right," or "There is some truth to that."

Some students react negatively to classes where the instructor encourages discussion and encourages students to develop their own views and answers. Their students protest, "I didn't pay good money to sit and listen to a bunch of uninformed people express their opinions. I can get that in any bar." This attitude is legitimate. It is also narrow minded.

The word *education* means to "draw out of." It does not mean "shovel into." A good education teaches you to think for yourself. It teaches you to ask good questions and then learn how to find the answers on your own. A good education does not give you a diploma for learning how to seek out an expert for any question you have. It teaches you how to both listen to authorities and come to your own conclusions.

Internal learners with a clear sense of self direction need and appreciate an instructor who will let them follow their own path. Such students get upset with instructors who tell them exactly what they must learn, and in what way. For them, too much course structure is abrasive. They feel handicapped more than helped. Such reactions are legitimate and narrow minded.

In every field of study, certain basics must be mastered. There are basic terms and concepts that must be understood. There are some techniques fundamental to the mastery of the subject even though the reasons why may not be given.

Being Both Internal and External in Learning

Students who get the most out of school are able to both follow the tightly-controlled steps used by some teachers and organize their own learning experiences when in a class taught by someone who gives few guidelines.

Conclusion and Suggestions

What do you do when a teacher is less than ideal? Do you get angry when you discover that you don't have a good match between yourself and the instructor?

By now we hope that you begin to realize, if you didn't know already, that finding a really good match between yourself and an instructor does not happen all the time. If one of your habits is to find something wrong with others, your instructors will give you plenty of opportunities. If you are an experienced victim, then the college will provide you with many chances to be upset, complain to classmates, and attack instructors you've judged to be imperfect.

As an alternative to being a victim, we have these suggestions:

1. Ask around before registration to find out who the more well-regarded instructors are. If you have a choice between instructors, you'll know which one to choose.
2. Try to get as much out of every course regardless of who your instructor is or how much the teaching style does not fit your preferred learning style. Be open to try a new way of learning.
3. When you have a problem understanding what is happening in a course, make an appointment to talk with the instructor. Be prepared to ask for what you want.
4. If you still have problems, go to the office or center that teaches studying and reading skills. The instructors there can be very helpful.

Action Review: Resolving Conflicts Between Teaching and Learning Styles

☐ When I dislike the way an instructor teaches do I look to see if we have a conflict between my learning style and the instructor's teaching style?

☐ If any of the following are descriptive of me do I take steps to compensate for my natural style in classes with instructors with different styles?

    auditory—visual
    right brain—left brain
    friendly—distant
    external direction—internal direction

☐ Have I examined my assumptions about instructors and developed a more realistic and tolerant attitude?

☐ When I encounter difficulty with the way an instructor teaches do I take steps to improve things?

Success Group Activity

Talk with each other about how conflicts between teaching styles and learning styles help explain difficulties you might have had with the way some instructors teach. Help each other develop a positive plan of action for handling future conflicts.

Talk about the assumptions students often make about college instructors and how you can modify your expectations to match reality better!

Chapter 13

How to Be Positive with Your Instructors and Salvage Poor Grades

Do you know that tracking positives gets more from instructors than tracking negatives?

Do you know that many students are unaware of the effects of their behavior on instructors?

Do you know that negative student behavior can lead to negative instructor behavior?

Do you know that it is possible to improve poor course work to get a good final grade?

How to Improve the Instruction You Get

Reward Good Instruction

When your instructors do things that you consider to be good teaching, be attentive, nod, smile, and compliment them. Instructors' actions can be influenced by the attention they receive from students. When you and the other students indicate your approval for your instructors' good teaching, you'll get more of what you like and less of what you don't like.

Provide Your Instructors with Feedback

If your instructors encourage periodic evaluations of their classroom performance, be sure to fill out their evaluations. Let your instructors know what you like! If you want to tell an instructor that there is something that needs to be improved, be sure to give an example of what you don't like and what you would like.

Prepare Good Questions Before Going to Class

As you read your assignments for class, decide what questions you would like to ask. Most instructors want students to ask good questions. When students sit back timidly, afraid to ask questions, instructors wonder whether or not the students have the least idea of what's going on.

Although our students have never claimed that reinforcing good teaching will turn an instructor from a Simon Legree into a Dale Carnegie, students who actively work to get better teaching are emphatic about the positive effect students can have on instructor performance.

☆ REMEMBER: positive student actions leads to positive instructor actions.

Negative Student Actions Can Lead to Negative Instructor Actions

College teaching can sometimes be disheartening. College professors are known to complain of unmotivated, uncaring, and ill-prepared students. The cause of the professor's distress is often negative student behavior.

Following are some examples of ways that students upset their professors. As you go through the list ask yourself:

Do I ever behave this way toward an instructor?
What effect would this behavior have on me if I were the instructor?
If I were the instructor, how would I respond to students who acted in such ways?

By taking the perspective of your instructor, you may appreciate how easily professors can become disheartened by nice students who simply aren't aware of what it's like to deal with well-meaning but unthinking students.

Actions That Irritate Instructors

Tell Emotional and Personal Stories Leading Nowhere

Students often become so involved with class discussions that they go off into personal stories which are of no value to anyone.
Useful alternative: Think about what you're going to say and why you're going to say it. Ask yourself "Will what I say be of value?"

Act Unhappy When Your Instructors Don't Perform Well

All of us have days when we'd prefer to avoid contact with other people. Professors cannot hide in a closet until a bad mood passes. Even when they are not at their best, they still have to show up.
Useful alternative: Show a little compassion. Don't expect the impossible. No one can be outstanding daily. If your professor appears to be having an off day, work your hardest to do everything possible to make the class a good one.

After class, if you liked your instructor's performance, go out of your way to let him or her know he or she did well. It's doubly important on tough days for instructors to know that they can ride out a storm.

Tell Other Students What You Dislike About the Instructor— Never Go Directly to the Instructor

It is easy for you to complain to other students about a particular instructor. The problem is that your complaints won't help your instructor teach better or your classmates learn more. Your complaints may result in students responding negatively toward your instructor, which will surely hurt his or her performance. Why make things tough for your instructor, your fellow students, and yourself?

> *Useful alternative*: Don't downgrade your instructors to other students. Try to help your instructors, not hurt them! Encourage yourself and other students to look for the good points in your instructors. As we've stated throughout this chapter, try to create a climate in which your instructors can do an even better job.

Ask Your Instructors to be Personal Counselors

It's natural for you to want to be friendly with your instructors. That's great! Unfortunately, some students expect too much of them. These students expect their instructors to be terribly interested in all of their personal ideas, interests, and problems. Most instructors want to be friendly with their students, but are not in a position to be personal counselors.

The difficulties begin to arise when students begin dropping in all the time to talk, unload about their personal problems, and generally cut into the rather tight schedules that many professors work within. Professors often feel uncomfortable discouraging drop-ins. Few professors want to be known as uncaring or uninterested in their students. Professors want the best for their students and are usually willing to try to help. It's simply unfair to ask professors to spend their time socializing on the job or solving your personal problems.

> *Useful alternative*: Try not to ask your instructors to do more than they are professionally equipped to handle. If you need help with personal problems, see the professional counselors at your college or talk to your best friends.

Demand That Your Instructors Give You Special Favors and Consideration

We've known students who will miss half of the semester, come in, and ask to borrow the instructor's lecture notes. We've known students who would ask instructors if they could take the midterm two weeks late because of a vacation trip.

Useful alternative: Most of your instructors will be people who are interested in your academic and personal well-being. Instructors understand that you may run into financial, transportation, health, family, and numerous problems which interfere with successful performance in class. Don't be afraid to let your instructor know when an event drastically alters your performance. If you're ill for two weeks with the flu, let your instructor know why you're missing class. Instructors like to know why a student isn't coming to class.

Handle minor problems yourself. If your car breaks down and you miss class, don't expect your instructor to repeat an entire lecture for you. Borrow notes from one or two people in the course, two is best since they will show discrepencies.

How to Turn A Bad Situation Around

If you are likely to receive a D or F in a course, you can often salvage a bad grade. But, you have to learn to be diplomatic and pleasant to deal with.

Avoid Failing Courses by Being Diplomatic and Willing to Work

Students having academic problems approach instructors with unbelievable stories when a straightforward approach is best.

Go talk to your instructor and ask for a chance to make up your work. *Go with a plan!* Offer to make up exams. Ask if you can write an extra paper or rewrite the project you threw together the night before it was due. Explain why you are willing to. Instructors are much more willing to give students a chance if they are willing to admit that they have done poorly and are willing to quickly turn over a new leaf.

One of my early "learning experiences" involved messing up on a mid-term exam. There was no make-up exam. I felt desparate. I wrote out three questions that could be used as the basis for writing long essays. Then I went to the instructor and asked if I could get extra credit for researching and answering one or more of the three questions. I said I would write my answers in the form of a paper using information from outside the textbook. I was delighted when he agreed to my request. I ended up with a B in the course. The results would have been different if I had not done the extra credit work. - MK

Most instructors will give you a chance. Bad grades are not permanent unless you allow them to be.

For example, if you do poorly on the mid-term or final, ask to take the make-up exam. Ask for a chance to show that you do know the material. (Maybe you didn't then but things have changed now.) Even if the instructor says you can't take the test to change your grade, ask to take it anyway to see for yourself if you can do better. Assuming that you will get a better score, this will have a psychological effect on the instructor later.

☆ WARNING: Don't just walk away from a class you do poorly in. Officially drop the class. A failing grade turned in at the end of the course becomes part of your permanent school record.

Consider Taking an Incomplete

If you anticipate a bad grade in a course because you haven't been able to get all of the work in, and you want to earn a good grade, then consider asking the instructor to submit an *incomplete* on the grade sheet. Your instructor can follow school policies that allow students to complete course work after the course is over. At most schools you have at least a year.

You can change the past if you want to. A sincere request for another chance, a specific plan about what you will do, and commitment to do it will influence the hardest of instructors and deans.

Instructors Are Human Too

The list of behaviors that frustrate instructors is not meant to convey the message that instructors are special people who have to be treated with kid gloves. Not at all. Instructors are human beings who react just as you do to pressures, demands, and problems.

What we're suggesting to you is the simple fact that you make a difference! You can either choose to help your instructors be better instructors who enjoy teaching or you can choose to behave in ways that cause instructors to be unhelpful and boring. Instructors who go around with a chip on their shoulders are often created by students who don't appear to care about their education.

The choice is yours. Accept the fact that you will have great instructors, mediocre instructors, and some who appear to be life's losers. Regardless, follow the suggestions we've made. Try to help every instructor be a good instructor. It's all up to you!

Action Project for Getting Better Teaching

1. Take some time with several classmates to develop a list of things that good teachers do. List specific, observable actions.
2. List all those things you might do that could be rewarding for an instructor.
3. Observe each instructor to see how much or how little of the desired teaching behaviors occur.
4. Compliment and reward instructors who do many of the things you list as good teaching. Be specific. Let instructors know what you appreciate. Remember: The more quickly you reward a desired behavior, the more effective your reward.
5. Observe how you react when a teacher is less than what you would like. Ask yourself, "Do I do any of the things that upset and frustrate teachers?"
6. Track positives. When an instructor is slow in giving you good teaching behaviors, look for any little signs of improvement and immediately reinforce the improvement.

7. Ask yourself, "Am I a rewarding person to have in class?" If you aren't, then here is a good chance to practice. Trite as it is, there is a lot of wisdom in the old idea of "An apple for the teacher!"

Success Group Activity

Talk about some of your past experiences with good instructors and poor instructors. Talk about youraelves as teachers. Have you had any teaching experiences as parents, supervisors or managers? How easy is it? What feedback and responses do you appreciate from people you are trying to teach?

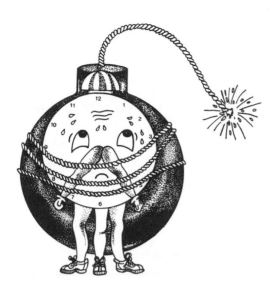

Chapter 14

How to Maintain
a Positive Attitude
in Stressful Situations

Do you know the difference between stress and strain?

Do you believe that the way for your life to get better is for other people to change?

Did you know that stress can be good for you?

Can you be both optimistic and pessimistic?

Do you know how to create a plan to decrease your negative experiences and increase your positive experiences?

Misunderstandings About Stress

Stress has received a bad name in recent years. People have the impression that stress is bad for you. It isn't. *Too much* stress is bad for you. A certain amount of stress is necessary for health and well-being.

Before we look at a simple and practical way to handle the many pressures that can build up on a college student who is working, raising a family and handling other important responsibilities, let's clarify some misunderstandings about stress:

1. Selye made a mistake

Much of the confusion and misunderstanding about stress traces back to Dr. Hans Selye, the physician who created the concept *biological stress* in 1936. He used the wrong term. In his memoirs he apologizes saying that when he came from Europe to attend medical school he did not understand the English language or physics very well. He said he should have named his concept the *strain syndrome*.

2. There is no stress in any situation until a person experiences strain

In physics a stressor is an external force attempting to deform an object. The effect on an object is measured as strain. Human beings differ so widely in their abilities to handle various situations, what is mildly challenging for one person is overwhelming for another.

3. Many people blame the situation for their reaction to it

It is not unusual to hear people claim that they have stressful jobs, stresses at home, or stresses as college students. That is a misperception. They are confusing the situation with their reaction to it. It isn't the circumstance that counts, it is your reaction to it that counts. What is stressful for one person is not stressful for another. An instructor that one student complains about for being extremely tough is appreciated by another for setting high standards.

4. A stressful situation can be beneficial

Selye coined the term *eustress* to emphasize that a certain amount of stress is necessary, is good for people. Athletes build up their physical strength through frequent workouts. Professional training programs build competence by straining people to their limits. Emotionally stressful experiences can motivate a person to learn new coping skills.

Stress Resistant and Stress Prone Personalities

Two people in identical situations have different reactions. Erma Bombeck is constantly amused about her experiences raising a family. Some mothers are so distressed trying to raise their families they need tranquilizers and psychiatric help.

Stress itself is not the problem. Stress is a concept that helps explain how and why some people become sick while others become strong in the same environment. A summary of research findings shows that:

Persons more likely to develop stress related illness:

- experience more stressors in routine activities;
- feel vulnerable, helpless, and without choices;
- have limited internal and external resources to draw on;
- feel socially isolated, not accepted;
- have little capacity for self-change; and
- accumulate memories of negative experiences.

Persons less likely to develop stress related illness:

- experience fewer stressors in routine activities;
- feel capable of taking effective action about upsetting events;
- draw action choices from a wide range of inner and external resources;
- experience family and friends as caring and supportive;
- manage self-change well; and
- convert negative experiences into beneficial learning.

How to Cope Effectively With Stressful Situations

Now that we've looked at some common misunderstandings about stress and reviewed what is known about people who handle pressures well, here is a practical course of action for coping effectively with stressful situations.

Clarify what is negative and stressful to you

Make a list of everything you experience as negative, upsetting, or stressful.

Sometimes the only way to be more positive is let yourself be negative. When you purposefully list all the things that you feel unhappy about you are not a negative person. You are a practical person taking the first step to coping effectively with many challenges. If you make yourself aware of all the forces working against you, you will be better prepared to hold up against them. By admitting that you are under stress and need steps to strengthen yourself, you will avoid burnout.

Discharge feelings, if necessary..

It is not unusual to experience some physical and emotional upsets when you start college for the first time. You may need to discharge your feelings. Some adult students report being more forgetful and irritable than usual and having periods of stomach and intestinal problems, sleeping difficulties, and headaches. These are normal reactions to stress. These symptoms usually prove to be temporary and should diminish fairly quickly if you find outlets for your feelings.

> Although I'm a pretty relaxed person most of the time, I did learn to recognize when stress was building up. I finally figured out that from time to time I would develop this overwhelming urge to clean the house, which meant that I was feeling too much pressure. I knew that things were really bad when the urge to clean the house changed and became specific—*I wanted to clean the refrigerator!*—MK

Go through your list, item by item, asking questions:

- Could I do something about this? How direct is my contact?
- What if I ignored this or avoided contact?
- Could I change the situation in some way? Who could help me?
- What if I changed my reaction to it?
- Why is this good for me?

The aim is to find ways to minimize the impact of the entire list. It isn't usually one big thing that does a person in, it is the accumulation of many little things. This action plan diminishes the total impact of things you experience as stressful. It also helps you feel more and control and less helpless.

Clarify what is positive and revitalizing for you.

Make a list of things you experience as positive in your life.
Ask yourself what activities make you feel happy and relaxed. What makes you feel good? Reflect on pleasant experiences.

Ask questions about how to repeat, increase, or have new positive experiences.

- Am I ignoring or taking for granted some positive aspects?
- What do I enjoy doing? What do I get enthusiastic about?
- What would I like to do that I keep putting off?
- With whom do I enjoy sharing good experiences?

Do a few things good for you to do.
It is important that you consciously engage in a self-nourishing selfishness. Psychologically healthy people are both unselfish and selfish. They act in ways that are good for their well being while still being helpful to others.

Highly Beneficial Activities

Laugh and Play With Friends
Successful people do not study all the time. Do anything you can

to prevent your college life from getting too serious, too burden-some, and too heavy.

Laughing and playing has many beneficial effects on your mental and physical health. Make a conscious effort to get into activities where you can yell or laugh or play hard and completely forget your responsibilities at school and home. If you are not doing much of this now, take another look at the recreation facilities on campus. Look for opportunities to do something just for yourself.

Get Physical Workouts

Do something several times a week in which you work up a sweat. This might be bike riding, jogging, playing raquetball or tennis, swimming, or perhaps just calisthenics or stretching in your room. In any case, doing something that increases your physical tiredness and helps you sleep better and rest better, which in turn helps you to study better.

Listen to Good Music

Play some classical music and do nothing else but listen to it. Don't try to exercise good time management by also shining your shoes, writing letters, or cleaning out your desk. Sit back and totally lose yourself in the music. The word "music" stems from the activity of musing. So do it. Muse.

Try Nap Therapy

Taking naps is a wonderful way to relax and revitalize yourself. If you have a car at school, try taking a nap in your car for ten minutes or so. Take a short nap early in the evening instead of watching television before studying. Take naps on weekends if you wish. Just because you're no longer a child doesn't mean that you can't benefit from a short nap now and then.

The Counseling Center Can Help

Most college students, at one time or another, feel lonely and depressed. If this happens to you, remember that such feelings are part of being human. School counselors can show you how to get through the unpleasant period while the natural emotional processes of self healing are operating.

Emotional upsets are a normal. You don't have to try to handle them alone. It is not a sign of strength to mask your feelings with drugs or put on a front of happiness. Emotional strength develops from feeling whatever you feel and talking to friends when things aren't working well. Get some help from your friends and other resources when things aren't so great.

Most counseling centers have useful books and cassette tapes on how to increase relaxation and reduce stress.

Outcomes

First, stress resistance can be learned. An effective plan of action eliminates and reduces negative, stressful experiences while adding and increasing positive, revitalizing experiences.

Second, when you understand that each stressful experience is your experience of some kind of strain, you avoid feeling vicitmized. You can use each strain like a workout. Just as lifting weights, biking, jogging, or swimming leads to getting physically stronger, using emotional strains as workouts leads you to becoming mentally and emotionally stronger.

It Isn't the Situation

What is stressful for one person is not stressful for another. If you avoid saying that your life would be better if only other people would change, and take positive steps to handle various negative experiences, the world you live in will have less and less stress. Martha Washington once observed:

> I am still determined to be cheerful and happy in whatever situation I may be, for I have also learned from experience that the greater part of our happiness or misery depends upon our dispositions and not upon our circumstances.

In the next chapter we will go beyond coping with negative situations. We will show how the people best at handling life's pressures gain strength from adversity and convert misfortune into good luck.

Action Review

☐ I have listed all the things I experience as negative, distressing or upsetting in my life.

☐ I have looked at each item on my list of distresses and developed plans for reducing, changing, avoiding, or minimizing them.

☐ I have listed what is positive and revitalizing for me.

☐ I have developed a plan for myself for increasingpleasant, revitalizing experiences.

☐ I understand that the feeling of distress is emotional strain and that strain can lead to getting stronger and better.

Success Group Activity

Talk about stresses and pressures you each feel. Ask each other "How do you manage?" Find out what you each do that is enjoyable, positive, and revitalizing.

Discuss your reactions to reading that an important step toward dealing with negative situations is to make a list being actively negative. Is it difficult to be negative? Easy?

Talk about how easy or difficult it is to engage in activities that mav seem to be selfish.

Chapter 15

The School of Life:
How to Develop
a Survivor Personality

Do you learn useful lessons from your everyday experiences?

Do you know how to learn what no one can teach?

Do you know that it is healthy to be paradoxical?

Do you understand how playfulness, intuition, humor, and creativity are related to being a survivor?

Tests in the School of Life

Some people handle life's challenges better than others. They cope well with adversity and can often convert a bad situation into good luck.

Here's a little test for you. Imagine that you are about 21 years old and have just been married. For your honeymoon you have rented a romantic old wooden cabin for a week in the hills in southern California.

At dawn the first morning a woodpecker lands on the roof and starts hammering away at the shingles. The second morning the noisy bird is back again at dawn and starts his jackhammer search for insects. Every morning at dawn you are awakened by the noisy woodpecker.

What would you do? Move out? Demand that the manager get rid of the bird? Ask for a shotgun? What?

This is a true story. The honeymooners were a playful, good natured young couple. He worked as an illustrator with Walt Disney studios. You may have heard of them. They are Gracy and Walter Lanz. They created the cartoon character Woody the Woodpecker on their honeymoon as their response to the pesky woodpecker that woke them up every morning.

What Makes a Survivor?

Do you ever think of yourself as a survivor? Before reading further about the survivor personality, look through the following lists. Check off the traits that you possess. Add any not listed in the spaces at the bottom.

☐	calm	☐	emotional
☐	trusting	☐	cautious
☐	strong	☐	gentle
☐	messy	☐	organized
☐	serious	☐	playful
☐	lazy	☐	hard-working

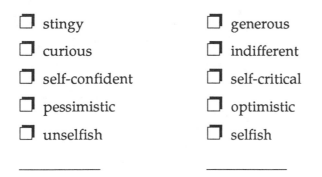

☐ stingy	☐ generous
☐ curious	☐ indifferent
☐ self-confident	☐ self-critical
☐ pessimistic	☐ optimistic
☐ unselfish	☐ selfish

_____ _____

_____ _____

It Isn't What You Are

Survival does not come from what you *are*, it results from how you *interact* with the world. The people who survive best interact flexibly. They adapt well to new situations. The more a person tries to think, feel, or act in a pre-set way, the lower the person's chances of surviving new challenges.

Flexibility and Adaptability

Successful coping comes from flexibility and adaptability. What makes flexibility possible? Being able to do both one thing and the opposite. It works like this—survivors are serious and playful; they are trusting and cautious; independent and dependent; they are selfish and unselfish; optimistic and pessimistic.

How can a person be both? People usually are thought of as one way or another, as introverted or extroverted, for example. Yet, many people with survivor personalities can be both introverted and extroverted.

Look at the checklists above. The more pairs of traits you recognized in yourself, the more likely it is that you have good survivor abilities. Two of the best signs would be, first, if you looked at the lists and quickly decided "All of the above." Second, would be if you wrote down several pairs of opposite qualities that you've noticed about yourself.

The list given above is not intended to bo complete. Its purpose is to make an important point. The more that pairs of paradoxical traits that are natural to you, the more flexible you are at dealing with any situation that develops.

Curiosity

In any difficult situation, it is essential, first, to be very open to quickly assess and understand what is occurring. Being open to quickly read, assess, and respond to whatever happens is an ingrained habit in life's best survivors.

Do you ask lots of questions? Want to know how things work? Wonder about the experiences others have had?

This sort of curiosity gives a person a mind that can deal with major challenges, unexpected developments, and bewildering situations. Life's best survivors are drawn to the unusual, the complicated, and the mysterious. Thus, when a difficulty develops, one that you have no experience with, the habit of being open to the new and unfamiliar predisposes you to quickly find out what is happening.

Playful Experimenting

The curiosity related to surviving has a certain quality to it. The person wants to know how things work. This is the life-long child who plays or experiments with almost anything. Laughing and delight when surprised or when something new is learned are typical reactions. Having fun in adversity is not uncommon.

A woman with two young sons had some medical tests done. The physician told her that she had an advanced stage of cancer and that she had a few months to live, a year at most.

She was shocked and distressed but as she drove home from the doctor's office she composed herself and decided that if she had only a year to live it would be the best year of her life. She stopped at a seafood market and purchased lobster tails for dinner. She made her family their favorite dessert.

In the weeks that followed she stopped doing all the things she should do but didn't enjoy. She constantly arranged to have happy, pleasant times with her boys and her husband.

That was over 17 years ago. Her cancer went away. Her sons are grown and married. She is now a proud grandmother.[1]

The Need to Have Things Working Well

The survivor personality is recognized by looking at what happens around a person. Things run better and go more smoothly when people with survivor personalities are involved. They are good to have around. This is the person you like to have along on a picnic. No matter what happens during the day, this person will deal with it easily in a pleasant way. You feel better being around them.

Surviving is an outcome with people who need to have things work well. From the first moment of quickly scanning a new and unexpected development, they expect things to turn out well.

In contrast, some people oriented themselves toward having things go wrong. They convert difficulties into the experience of being victimized. When problems develop, victims respond to the circumstances so that they can get people to feel sorry for them and pity them for having such a tragedy occur.

Needing to have things work well is a part of being constantly open to new and better ways of doing things. Old assumptions and beliefs may be changed or given up. Thus, another aspect of asking questions is to confirm how accurate your knowledge is. When a better way of perceiving or doing things comes along, people with survivor personalities adopt them.

Accurate Creativity

The ability to survive situations depends upon being able to read them accurately. Reading situations accurately results from having a nonjudgmental way of viewing the world. A judgmental attitude is to quickly condemn or find something wrong at the first impression. Judgmental thinking is to quickly view things as right or wrong, to quickly think of people as being good or bad.

To be creative is to come up with unusual ideas that work. By understanding the relationship between nonjudgmental thinking and creativity, the survivor pattern becomes more clear. People with the survivor personality are very complex. You're never quite sure what they are going to do in any situation. Yet, because they are adaptable, playful, non-judgmental, and have the intention of having things work out well, their solutions are often creative.

Intuition

Creativity is associated with awareness of subtle inner feelings. Sometimes survivors sense that something is wrong without knowing what it is. A tight stomach or an uneasy feeling can alert them. These feelings can be set off by anything—a person's tone of voice, something not said, a group's quietness, anything at all that doesn't fit.

The ability to read and respond to subtle inner feelings gives survivors an ability to follow hunches. In general, women are better at this than men. Women are known for their intuition. This is no accident, because women are usually raised with emotions a natural part of their lives.

Empathy

The people who survive best in a variety of situations have empathy for others. They can quickly read the emotional states, attitudes, and perceptions of others. They can step outside of their own feelings and perceptions to take into account the feelings and perceptions of others, even when disliked.

The empathy of survivors is not that of a weak, easily hurt bleeding heart. It is at times like the empathy that Abraham Lincoln used when he acted as a defense attorney. He was very successful because he would begin his opening statements to the jury presenting a better case against his client than the opposing attorney was able to do!

Empathy can include having an understanding for people who live and think in disliked ways. The attitude present in the empathy described here is "whether I enjoy you or dislike you, I am going to understand you as well as you understand yourself—and maybe better."

Defend Well

Sensitivity to others must be protected by toughness, however. This world has more dangers than just physical ones. Survival can depend on being able to defend yourself against emotional attacks, con jobs, emotional abuse, manipulations, and a whole range of hurtful or energy draining-things that some people do to others.

Strong feelings of self-esteem are essential for defense against hurtful people. Self-esteem acts like a nice padding so that what others say or think cannot penetrate.

The paradox is that the better the survivor becomes at shrugging off attacks or threats, the less others will try to attack. Ask anyone who has achieved black belt status in the martial arts. They find that after years of training to handle attackers, no one picks a fight with them!

Self-Managed Learning

The survivor personality can be learned but it cannot be taught. All significant learning is based on experience. You manage your learning by asking questions and developing answers. To view life as a school means to ask questions such as:

How did they do that?
Why didn't this work?
Why did I do that?
I wonder why people do such things?
What would happen if...?

Sometimes your best lessons are learned from bad experiences. You might ask questions such as

Next time, what will I do differently?
The next time that occurs, how will I handle it?
The next time a person says that to me, what will I say?

Go Beyond Your Teachers

A good education teaches you how to manage your own continuing development. Good teachers will show you how to go beyond their teaching. The real excitement in learning comes when you move past the level where others can tell you what you should learn or know. Much of the excitement of being fully alive as an adult is to recapture some of the wonderful curiosity that you used to feel as a child.

Serendipity

The word serendipity was coined by Horace Walpole. It describes an ability that some people have for turning accidents or misfortune into good luck. Serendipity usually starts with questions such as:

What can I learn from this?
Why is it good that this happened?
What do I have to do to make things turn out well?

If you can look back on a rough situation that you have gone through and appreciate that it was good for you that it happened, then you know what serendipity is all about. It is the ability to find something good in bad experiences.

Humor Can Make the Difference

The ability to laugh and joke during a crisis is very practical. Laughing has a direct effect on one's ability to solve problems efficiently and deal with situations. Examples can be seen on television or in the movies. Alan Alda playing Hawkeye in the television series *M.A.S.H.* was an excellent example. Erma Bombeck and Bill Cosby react to life's events with the humor typical of people with survivor personalities.

Why does humor help? Laughing reduces tension. Creative problem solving, accurate thinking, and good physical coordination are best in moderate emotional states. In athletics, the coach of a football team wants the linemen worked up to a high emotional state. In sports such as basketball, tennis, or baseball, a more moderate level of emotional arousal leads to better performance.

The humor used by survivors is directed toward the immediate situation. It is aimed at playing with the situation and poking fun at it. It is as though the person has the attitude, "I am bigger than this situation. This is my toy. I am going to play with it."

The person seems to be asking, "How does this look from a different point of view? What would happen if I turned it upside down? What if the reverse were true? What unusual things exist here?" By playing with the situation and toying with it, the person keeps from being overwhelmed and at the same time is likely to come up with a way to survive.

It Isn't the Event, It's Your Reaction to It

People with survivor personalities rarely remain upset about what has been lost. They do not remain distressed when things have gone bad. They focus on the future. They know that nothing can be done now about what has happened. They accept responsibility for turning things around. They accept reality as it is. They accept responsibility for their reactions to conditions.

In the opening chapter we emphasized being responsible for yourself. Throughout the book, whenever we addressed a difficult situation, our approach has been to show you how you can handle the difficulty in a way that makes you a stronger, more capable person. Our aim has been to show you how to be a life-long learner.

When you graduate from school you go through a ceremony called *commencement*. Commencement means to begin. Succeeding in college is only one step toward success in the school of life. Have you commenced?

Action Review: Indicators of Survivor Personality Qualities

☐ Do I feel comfortable being paradoxical?

☐ Is my self-esteem strong enough that I'm not too vulnerable to criticisms or failures?

☐ Am I known to be a playful, curious person?

☐ Am I a good person to have in charge? Am I good at making things work well?

☐ Can I count on my hunches and intuition?

☐ Am I good at reading other people? Do I have good empathy skills?

☐ Do I defend myself effectively when attacked?

☐ Do I learn good lessons from daily experiences?

☐ Am I able to turn misfortune into good luck?

Success Group Activity

How many times have you noticed that you are one way at one time but just the opposite at another? Talk with each other about your reaction to learning that it is desirable to be paradoxical.

Tell each other about one of the worst experiences you've gone through in your life and what you've learned or gained from it. Answer the question "Why was it good that this happened?" Take your time with this. Let each person finish completely before anyone else starts with their story.

Appendix A

Career Choice, Career Change

Do you know what the word *vocation* means? It means to find a life's work that *calls* to you. Finding a career that suits you can take time. Until you find your calling in life you may feel uncertain, confused and lost. These are normal feelings. Almost everyone has them.

You probably have many positive feelings, too. Would you like to discover work that satisfies you? Brings excitement? Challenges your potential? Lets you meet the day with happy expectations? Allows the lifestyle you desire? Fine. Career counselors have many ways to help you discover an exciting new career path.

To begin your vocational discovery process you need to look at the kind of person you are, look at what you want from life, and look at the job market.

Values Change

The OTA students know there are many things they can do like maintaining a home, working on an assembly line or in a restaurant, and changing the oil in a car. But what is it that you choose to spend your life energies on for the next 10 to 20 years? To start to answer this question, you must examine what you value in life. The older you get, the more your career decisions will be based on your values.

Some of the values people bring to work are:

- Helping people or making the world a better place.
- Being the boss, having power, influence over others.
- Having security, work well understood, steady paycheck.
- Having excitement, challenge, and pressure.
- Making money enough to live the good life.
- Being allowed to choose own time, work, standards.
- Bringing beauty, variety, new ideas into the world.

Other satisfactions in your work other than money include:

- Working with things or information rather than people.
- Being in a nice place, wearing good clothes.
- Having physical activity and working out-of-doors.
- Working as a member of a friendly team.
- Performing a service of value to others.

Now take a moment to reflect on jobs you have had in the past. What were the qualities you really liked or valued? What were the things you could do without?

Your values change a great deal with various life cycles and changes of circumstances. A man of 50, who has been bumped from the middle management of the company to which he has devoted 25 years, will feel differently than he did starting a career. It may be that being a company man is much less important than being his own man. For a woman who loses her partner and her financial security at the same time, security may be her highest value as she struggles to survive.

Transferable Skills

Each one of us has many skills. You may be good at communication, juggling figures, fixing things with your hands, or being sensitive to people's needs. First, identify what your skills are. Let your friends help. Then decide which skills you would like to use or emphasize in your next career.

Some skills that business and industry value the most are:

Budget management
Supervising
Public relations
Handling deadline pressure
Negotiating/arbitrating
Communicating
Getting along with people
Interviewing
Instructing
Information gathering

More important than knowing what the working world wants is knowing what you want. You can see that the journey to a new career starts inward when you question, "What do I value in life? What have I got to offer? Which skills do I choose to use in my next career?" No one can really answer these questions for you. Various assessing methods can help sift and clarify values, skills, and interests. The decision is yours.

Some Vocational Assessment Instruments

The following instruments are available through many college Testing Departments. Usually testing requires a counselor referral.

Strong-Campbell Interest Inventory—SCII

An occupational interest inventory comparing students' answering patterns with those of people satisfactorily employed in various occupations. Questions deal with likes/dislikes; norms based on a population of four-year degree, professional employees. Probably more suited to students with interest in professional fields requiring at least a four-year degree. (Based upon John Holland's research.)

Career Assessment Inventory—CAI

Similar in format to the Strong-Campbell. Normed on general population. Usually more suitable for students in vocational education.

Self-Directed Search—SDS

Self-evaluating, less formal inventory; written by John Holland. Categories cover areas of interest and competencies.

Minnesota Importance Questionnaire—MIQ

Vocational inventory in which test takers are asked to rank job statements; thus indicating features important to their ideal job. Assists in prioritizing values and predicting job satisfaction.

California Occupational Preference System—COPS

A self-administered and self-scored inventory, comparing relative strength of interest in many different occupations. Provides print-out of college majors. Available for different reading levels.

Myers-Briggs Type Indicator , Edwards Personal Preference Schedule , Personality Research Form—PRF

These are personality profiles, indicating personality types. They help to understand how students perceive information and life.

Personality Mosaic

Inventory from which student can obtain Holland Code (as in Strong-Campbell, etc.) and data/people/things rating.

Please Understand Me—Kiersey & Bates
(Jefferson software)

Results are similar to Myers-Briggs Personality Profile. Can be completed on the Apple computer, or with pencil and paper. Used primarily as self-awareness tool.

Study Skills: Self-Exploration in Series 3
(Software available for Apple Computers, Educational Media Corp.)

Identifies your learning style to maximize your efforts.

System of Interactive Guidance and Instructions—SIGI

Computerized occupational assessment and exploration system in nine steps. Usually first section can be completed in approximately two hours.

What Are Your Fun Interests?

People's values change, but certain traits of personality stay the same. What do you know about your own nature?

Do you like to be left alone while you work with your hands or at something mentally challenging? Are you spurred on when you have a chance to lead others?

Do you like work where you can enjoy being around people and feel more alive when you work as a team member? What do you do in your spare time that is fun? In the spaces following write down what you know about yourself:

A Self-Assessment

My top work values:

_____

_____

_____

My top job satisfiers (other than money):

_____

_____

_____

The transferable skills I want to use on my next job:

_____

_____

_____

My fun interests are:

_____

_____

_____

Occupations that might be a good match for me are:

_____

_____

_____

Now that you have looked at who you are and what you want, it is time to examine possible careers. It is useful to have three or four careers in mind as a matter of comparison. If you do not know of someone who has that career, ask job placement, counseling/ career department or an instructor in that field to help you identify a resource person for an information interview.

The three most important rules for getting job information are:

1. *Talk* to people!
2. Talk to *people*!!
3. *Talk to people*!!!

How to Get First-Hand Career Information

Job market information changes so rapidly that by the time it gets into books, it is often two years old and out of date. Magazines and computerized information systems have more current data about careers. For the most up-to-date word on occupations, there is no better way than to talk to people. A general feel for the wide market flow can be obtained in casual contacts with people and from conducting self-arranged information visits.

Guidelines for Information Interviewing

• Arrange to visit a work place where people are doing the

kinds of jobs that you have an interest in.
- Never ask for a job.
- You can go by yourself or with a small group.
- Give a professional appearance: clean, careful, conservative, classic.
- Wear comfortable shoes; you may be given a tour.
- Do not walk around or snoop where you are not wanted.
- Come prepared to take notes; be a good reporter; get the facts.
- Stay within your timelines.
- Ask only those questions that are of most importance to you.
- Make sure you know to whom you are talking.
- Be a good listener.
- Take a real interest in the person, the field, and the organization.
- Share some things about yourself.
- Ask if you can stay in contact with the person.
- Always get referrals of other people to whom you may talk.
- *Always* send a thank you note.

Questions to Ask Regarding the Career
- What are the training/degree requirements for this line of work?
- What is the best way to enter this field to ensure advancement?
- Which entry-level jobs are best for learning as much as possible?
- What is the starting salary for a person in this field?
- Are there extra social/professional obligations that go with this work (unions, professional organization meetings, etc.)?
- What sort of changes are happening in this occupation that will affect future opportunities?
- Who are some people I should talk with to learn more about this career?
- Are there any special considerations for women/men starting in this field?
- Do you need special tools or equipment in this field?

- Are there any occupational hazards in this line of work?

Career Markets

You have started the journey inward, looking at what is true for you. You have examined values, satisfiers, skills interests and career options. Now it is time to explore the day-to-day work world and eventually hitch your wagon to the future.

Sources of information about career markets, national and local:

Newspapers
Weekly news magazines: *U.S. News & World Report, Business Week*
Monthly magazines: *Fortune, Money*
Business section of newspapers
In-house papers and newletters for employees
Chamber of commerce publications
Local magazines
Professional and trade journals
Civil service offices

For labor market predictions:

Occupational Outlook Handbook
CIS Occupational Information

☆ The classified section of a newspaper lists *less than* 20% of the available jobs. It is best used to survey the job market for shortages of employees in certain fields, not for a comprehensive job information. For the best and most current market and job information, talk to people, talk to people, *talk to people!*

Pay Attention to Future Trends

No crystal-ball gazer can guarantee job security in the 1980s, 1990s, or the year 2000. Changes in population, energy sources, and 29% of those entering the work force will be minorities.

technology, environment, and social values are causing a decline in some occupations, an increase in other occupations, and the birth of new occupations.

We are no longer on a local/national economy but a global/ outer space economy that will require cooperation and communication like never before.

The present shift from a manufacturing society to an information society will be more drastic than our shift from horse and buggy to the assembly line.

Our increasing population will see people living in parts of the world presently considered uninhabitable. The lengthening life span will lead to major social changes.

No matter how carefully we study the trends of the future, there will be some occurrences, inventions, and surprises that are totally unpredictable, will affect your life profoundly, and will take a great deal of flexibility and adaptability on your part. Nourishing that part of you that looks on change as exciting and rewarding will pay big dividends. Be a survivor! The average person will change their career three times in their life.

The world's population will double in 35 years. About 90% of all scientists in our history were alive in 1970. Energy consumed in the last 100 years equals one-half of all the energy consumed in the last 2,000 years. Computer jobs will grow by 30,000 every year. There will be 17,000 more engineering positions than people to fill them. Medical workers will increase by over 25% by 1990. Two-thirds of American workers will be employed in services rather than products by 1990.

Retraining and educational benefits will become as important to employees as wages. More women will combine career and home interests, resulting in increased need for child-care services. Seventeen percent of all workers will be in the health or education field, and there will be jobs in the health, energy, and information industries that do not yet exist. The new business person, with good ideas and the energy to implement them, will have great opportunity in the future. World trade with Asia, Australia and Spanish-speaking countries will be bigger business. By the year 2000 only 8% of the jobs will be in manufacturing, 90% in services,

No crystal ball can guarantee a path to job security. We can, however, make ourselves highly valued employees by keeping ready for change by continued education. American businesses are spending billions of dollars to educate and train their employees. Seeking new opportunities to learn, getting excited over new ideas, and welcoming a chance for more training will be among the most valued traits of an employee. The thing we know for sure about the future and careers is it will bring change and challenge.

For Further Information

For further information and materials on obtaining career information and the information interview, see:

The Complete Job Search Handbook by Howard Figler
Go Hire Yourself an Employer by Richard Irish
Who's Hiring Who by Richard Lathrop
Bernard Haldane Associates Job & Career Building by Richard
    Germann
Job Hunting by Charlie Mitchell and Lauren Collins
What Color Is Your Parachute? by Richard Bolles

Blazing New Trails

As you look for a new career, remember that you are a pioneer. A few years ago people did not change careers. They stayed in the same jobs all their lives, even when they felt bored and dissatisfied.

You are on an exciting new adventure. The lack of clear direction about what to do is an opportunity, not a stumbling block. Searching for a second or third career, starting a first career after raising a family, is a new development for working people.

You are cutting a new path into new territory. Help and resources are available, but finding a satisfying vocation is up to you. So dream about a future that appeals to you and go for it!

Appendix B

The Authors Talk

A: Bernadine, now that we've completed the book I'd like to ask you some questions.

B: Sure Al, what are they?

A: You started college many years after high school. You had five children to raise. What motivated you to go to college?

B: I remember looking out the window one day and thinking that I've got everything in my life that a woman is supposed to want and need—I'm married, I had a nice home, I had children. How come I'm not satisfied?

A: What happened?

B: I searched around asking, "What else is there? What's missing from my life?" There was so much I didn't know about. I intended to write articles for magazines but I kept bumping up against my own ignorance. I wondered why anybody would want to listen to me say anything. I felt it was time to learn more about the many things I didn't know.

A: What got you to college?

B: A neighbor got me to college. I was too afraid to do it all by myself. A neighbor up the road had been taking a writing class and said "Bernadine, if I can do it, you can do it." I was too nervous and scared to go by myself but I went with her.

A: You had no college courses before this?

B: No credit college courses. I had ventured into the non-credit courses, some creative writing courses, that sort of thing.

A: How long had it been since you were in high school?

B: Seventeen years.

A: A long time since you'd done any studying or taken any tests.

B: Oh yes, a very long time. The idea of being tested was scary.

A: When you started back to college, did you have any kind of program in mind or were you just exploring?

B: I was simply exploring. I decided to take something I was interested in that wouldn't be too much over my head.

A: What was that?

B: History. I always liked history. To me it was like a story of people. I always liked stories. So I took a history course.

A: You have a master's degree in counseling and work with the older students. How did you get from taking a history class to the work you're doing now?

B: I kept taking one step at a time with that same history teacher as my advisor. He kept saying, "Take transfer courses," and at that time I didn't even know what transfer courses were, but trusted his good judgment and followed his advice.

A: You are well known for being good at helping older students handle their fears when they come back to college. How did you come to specialize in that? Why do you put so much of your time into that?

B: Because I'll never forget being sweaty palmed, shaky-kneed, and scared spitless. The day that I went down to register for my first class I had to drive on the freeway for the first time to get to the registration location. When I walked in it seemed there was this sea of young faces around, it was not common then to be an older woman going back to school. They looked at me and assumed I must be a teacher and must know what I was doing. I knew that I sure didn't. Now I know that my fears were based on false assumptions, but back then I felt I didn't have a brain left.

B: I'm curious about you, Al. You said you were raised by a working mother. That you learned to be independent very early. I worried about my children—would I be taking time away from them when they needed me. How did you feel as a child being raised by a working mother?

A: It was just something that we all had to adapt to. My father died when I was in grade school. I was between seventh and eighth grades. My sister was almost five years younger. When he first got ill and couldn't work, my mother obtained a job as a ward clerk at a hospital nearby.

B: How long was he ill?

A: About a year. After he died, Mom sat us down and explained that we all had to pitch in and take care of ourselves. She said I was old enough that if I wanted spending money I had to find ways to earn it—which meant a paper route, mowing lawns, and doing odd jobs around the neighborhood.

B: Your mother's going to work was a necessity. There was no question in your mind that this was the way things had to be.

A: Right, it had to be that way. A couple of years later, one of the physicians at the hospital had seen that my mother was very capable and urged her to better herself. She looked around and signed up for courses that would give her secretarial skills. She started going to night school while my sister and I were still relatively young.

B: What was your sister's reaction about being left and your mother's working? What does she remember about this?

A: It was lonely at times but we managed okay. We're a very independent family. We took care of ourselves. I was old enough so that when my sister came home from school, I would be there to watch out for her. We took care of ourselves when mother was at night classes. To practice her typing and shorthand she would often wait until we were in bed and then stay up late practicing her lessons. That, or get up early in the morning and practice before she'd go to work.

B: You had a role model of your mother not only working, but of going to school to improve her skills.

A: I guess you could say that. My sister went back to college after raising her family. She now has a master's degree in communications. We sometimes speak to groups of older students who are starting college and we tell our story about how they shouldn't feel guilty. They can ask their kids to help out.

B: In what way?

A: My mother explained that she was no longer going to do all the laundry. If I wanted clean, ironed pants to wear to high school, I had to wash and iron them myself. I was old enough and capable enough to do that. I accepted that and did it.

B: We did the same in our family. I'm from a very large family and the division of labor was a necessity. I can remember my brother pressing his pants and ironing his shirts. I had two role models in my family. My mother showed me in the home that jobs could be delegated as in any successful business. My father was also a role model. He had been raised on a farm in Illinois. His father told him at the end of the sixth grade he had enough education and had to work on the farm. My father didn't continue his education until after he was twenty-one and moved away. Dad gave his young working years to his family, but then picked up his education again. He became a lawyer. He went to night school and worked full time during the day. Both my mother and father showed me that having high expectations of yourself can make you a better member of a successful family.

A: So it does help—this is the point that you make in the book—how it can be a gift to your children to let them see that education is something that is very important, that it's worth putting the time and effort into.

B: Children may not necessarily recognize that this is a gift right off. I can remember that my son balked a bit about Mom going back to school. But one time when he was in trouble with a history assignment that he had neglected to do and put off, I was able to give him a short synopsis of the Civil War in an hour or two and he got his paper in. From that day on he saw some value in education. I asked my girls, now that they're grown up, if they saw a big difference in the way the household was run or if they felt deprived in any way when I went back to school. Their response was, "Gee, Mom, you've always been busy and involved in doing things so we didn't see where it was all that different. We always shared the load of the housework." And that's true, they did.

A: I would agree. Neither my sister nor I felt deprived. We weren't upset. We adapted to the situation and handled it well. To this day we are a very close family with a great deal of respect for each other.

B: You talk in the book, Al, about getting the family's support behind you. I think it's wonderful when that happens. My husband was very supportive of my going back to school. He always told the children, "Mom has to study now," or "You can do that yourself," That support was very important. We were all very proud when graduation day rolled around for me. It had been a family affair and everyone felt proud.

A: How long did it take you from the time when your neighbor got you to go, shaky and nervous, to sign up for your first class until you graduated with your master's degree?

B: About nine years. I got a bachelor's degree in education in five years, and taught for three years after that. I then went on for another two years for my master's degree.

A: If a person had walked up to you and said I predict that nine years from now you will have a master's degree and be employed at a college doing a valuable service teaching older students, what would you have said?

B: "You've got to be kidding! I can't even envision myself getting a degree!" I could not have envisioned myself being competent enough in any subject that I could stand up in front of a class and teach somebody something in a college setting. That was totally foreign to the way I felt inside. Nobody could have told me when I first started those classes that I would be spending six years of my life in higher education. No one could have convinced me of that. That's why I don't try selling my returning students on a degree program right away. It's "Can I get through this first term? Can I get through this first class?" They have to have their confidence in their academic ability reinforced before they can widen their vision and even consider a degree program.

A: So here you are now, you not only graduated, but you became a teacher, and now you talk to many groups of people.

B: I can remember looking at that very first history teacher I had. He'd come in and would put his lecture notes on the podium and not even give them a glance, but just roll out with 45 minutes of this exciting, interesting information delivered in a positive manner. I wondered how a person gets to that point. One day I asked him. He said, "You know your subject." Now I can look at the fact that I know returning older students really well so I don't have any problem standing in front of an audience talking about the fears and barriers for returning OTA students.

A: You start out on a path. Later you look back and you realize how far you've come, but at the beginning of the path there's no way you can know how far you will go. So the key to the whole thing is to start on the path and take it one step at a time. Keep taking the steps.

B: Yes! What about you? What was the big step for you?

A: My path was much different. I trace it back to when it was time for me to go to kindergarten when I was 4-1/2 years old. My mother insisted that I go although I didn't want to. I obeyed my mother, I went to school. The problem is, no one ever told me to stop. Finally, when I finished the twenty-third grade they said there's no more school.

B: Did you feel like you didn't know what to do with your life at that point?

A: As a matter of fact, I returned home and got a job as gardener. I worked for a year as a gardener. I was tired of reading books and having ideas put into my head. I needed a year to just let it all mellow while I worked at outdoor physical labor. It was like taking a sabbatical from books, colleges, and universities. During that year I started wondering what is it that I know that would be useful for people.

B: What did you decide to do?

A: I set off in several directions. I started offering practical psychology workshops for people. I started my survivor personality research because of my experience in the paratroopers, being around combat survivors, and I started writing materials for college students that would help them handle college well. My background prepared me well for understanding the process of learning and how people learn.

B: You included a lot of that in the book.

A: Yes, what we have in our book is a blend of learning how to learn, along with the attitudes that good survivors have towards challenging situations. Life's best survivors are outstanding learners. They constantly learn lessons. They manage their own learning in the school of life. That's why they get better and better as the years go by.

B: I think that people who take time out for living before they go on to get more formal education have a real advantage because they bring some life experience to the learning process. They already know things about themselves and that they can survive. Then they can apply that knowledge as they go on to the process of growing.

I asked the same question you did. "What do I have that is useful to someone?" I was in an automobile accident that aggravated some problems. You gardened for a year. I was in bed for a year. During that year, I decided to change my life. I got to the same point. I asked "What have I got that I can still use?" "What talents do I have that will be of use to someone else?" I began critiquing manuscripts for people. I had done some writing and I thought "There's a bit of talent that I can use even when I'm lying on my back." It was during that year that I decided to go on and get my master's degree in counseling. I figured I could do that lying down or sitting up.

A: Yes, and that's what this book is all about. What I like is that the people who are the best survivors are the better people. They look for ways to make things work well for both themselves and others. It's a wonderful spirit. It's part of getting both older and younger. I've always liked the quote from Abraham Maslow that "no one becomes fully self-actualized until they are at least 60."

B: As I teach more and more of the older students, some much older than average, and as they teach me in the classroom, I find that it's a wonderful experience, this exchange that they bring. I would hate to have a classroom that had people of only 18, 19, 20 or 30. I really like the mixture of age and experience in a community college because that's what makes for a rich teaching-learning atmosphere.

A: It's really satisfying to participate in the learning that is taking place. People are learning; their lives are getting better. I find that it's a very rewarding activity. It's very satisfying.

B: To see the people that refuse to stop at any age. And when you see them at 65, 75, 80 years of age still being excited about the process, it's wonderful to be involved in that. They are thrivers. I get so much for myself as I help them in the growing process.

A: I do, too. And now you've helped write the book you wished you would have had when you started college?

B: Yes. It would have helped me a lot. I'm happy that others don't have to go through everything alone the way I did!

NOTES, REFERENCES, SUGGESTED READING

Chapter 2

1. A good book on this subject is *Paying for Your Education: A Guide for Adult Learners.* Copies may be purchased from College Board Publication Orders, P.O. Box 2815, Princeton, NJ 08541.

Chapter 3

1. Ekstrom, Ruth B., Harris, Abigail M., and Lockheed, Marlaine E.; *How to Get College Credit for What You Have Learned as a Homemaker and Volunteer.* Princeton, NJ: Educational Testing Service.

2. Carol Sasaki, assisted by many volunteers, now publishes *The HOME Door Newsletter,* with up-to-date information about ways to finance a college education. For a sample copy send $1 to: HOME, 6310 Riverside Drive, Dublin, OH 43017. To read more about Carol Sasaki, see "From Welfare to Work Force" by Chris Phillips in *Family Circle,* Oct. 11, 1988.

3. Hechinger, Grace; "Will Your Company Pay for Your Classes?" *Glamour Magazine,* Feb. 1987.

Chapter 5

1. Mendelsohn, Pam; *Happier by Degrees.* (New York: Dutton, 1980). This is a practical book for women in college who have families. Mendelsohn includes 14 case histories of women who went back to school. She covers such topics as: how stu-

dent mothers become better mothers; how husbands and children react and think; juggling roles; being a single parent; and even some advice from husbands of reentry students to other husbands.

Chapter 6

1. Conroy, Mary; "Co-operative Education: Learn-and-Earn College Programs." Better *Homes & Gardens*, May 1987.

2. Eliason, Carol; "Co-op Can Make A Difference to Fledgling Entrepreneurs." Journal: *Workplace Education*, Sept.-Oct. 1984.

Chapter 8

1. Lakein, Alan; *How to Get Control of Your Time and Your Life* . (New York: New American Library, 1973). Using many practical examples drawn from his years as a time management consultant, Lakein shows how to establish priorities for yourself. The tips in his book show you how to choose activities that are of highest value to you and minimize the amount of time you put into low payoff endeavors. If your school has a large audiovisual library, it may have a copy of the film on this book. If you want to improve your time management, take a few friends and arrange to preview the film.

Chapter 10

1. "Relieving Anxiety in Classroom Examinations" by W. J. McKeachie, Donald Pollie, and Joseph Speisman. *Journal of Abnormal and Social Psychology*, Vol. 50, No. 1, January 1955, pp. 93-98.

Chapter 11

1. Strunk, William, Jr., and White, E. B.; *The Elements of Style* (New York: MacMillan, 1972). This book can be valuable to

any person wanting to improve the quality and clarity of their written communications. Buy a copy and hang onto it. This shows how to use good grammar, punctuate correctly, and write clearly.

Chapter 15

1. For more information about people who survive what they were told were terminal illnesses, read *Love, Medicine, and Miracles* by Bernie Siegel (New York: Harper and Row, 1986). Note: Chapter 8 includes a summary of Al Siebert's survivor personality research findings and self-healing.

Appendix A

1. Levinson, P.J.; *The Seasons of A Man's Life*, (New York: Knopf, 1978).

2. Porcino, Jane; *Growing Older, Getting Better: A Handbook for Women in the Second Half of Life*, (Reading, MA: Addison-Wesley, 1983).

WEEKLY SCHEDULE

HOUR	SUN	MON	TUES	WED	THURS	FRI	SAT
7-8							
8-9							
9-10							
10-11							
11-12							
12-1							
1-2							
2-3							
3-4							
4-5							
5-6							
6-7							
7-8							
8-9							
9-10							
10-11							
11-12							

INDEX

160

ACKNOWLEDGMENTS

This book is the result of the contributions of many people. We wish to express our special thanks to:

Timothy L. Walter for his many contributions to the early development of material in this book.

The instructors and counselors at Portland Community College for their encouragement, feedback, information, and suggestions.

Mary Tooley and Marcia House for their excellent professional secretarial skills and dedication to the project.

The students and readers who critiqued the early versions of the manuscript and provided us with valuable feedback.

Terry Rosen for her artistic skills, creativity, and extra efforts to bring the project to completion.

George Vaterneck for many years of supportive mentoring.

James V. McConnell for setting high standards as a teacher and writer.

Wilbert J. McKeachie and the University of Michigan psychology department faculty for creating a climate of professionalism in teaching.

John Gardner, Stuart Hunter, and the other Freshman Year Experience staff at the University of South Carolina for their dedication, vision, and excellent stewardship.

Our families for their years of support and appreciation.

FEEDBACK REQUEST

We'd like to know how *Time For College* has helped you. We would also welcome your comments, constructive criticism, or suggestions on how the book might be improved. Please write to us c/o:

Practical Psychology Press
P.O. Box 535
Portland, OR 97207

Ordering Extra Copies

To purchase a copy of *Time For College*
send $12.95 plus $1.00 for postage and handling to:

> Order Department
> Practical Psychology Press
> P.O. Box 535
> Portland, OR 97207

Also available:

Instructors Manual by Bernadine Gilpin for instructors
using *Time For College* as a textbook. Send requests to the
address above.

The OTA Childrens' Coloring Book by Teresa Rosen; 24
pages, full size. Send $2.95 plus $1.00 for postage and
handling to the address above.

Time For College can be obtained on cassette tape for
persons who are print handicapped by contacting:
> Recordings For The Blind
> 20 Roszel Road
> Princeton, NJ 08540
> 1-800-221-4792